A Practical Step-by-Step Guide to

COMPLETE
CONTAINER
GARDENING

A Practical Step-by-Step Guide to

COMPLETE
CONTAINER
GARDENING

WHITECAP BOOKS

4884
This edition published in 1997 by Whitecap Books Ltd.,
351 Lynn Avenue North Vancouver, B.C., Canada V7J 2C4
© 1997 CLB International, Godalming, Surrey
All rights reserved.

Printed in Singapore
ISBN 1-55110-509-8

Credits

Compiled by: Ideas into Print
Arrangements for hanging baskets and windowboxes: Jenny Hendy
Photographs: Neil Sutherland
Typesetting: Ideas into Print and Ash Setting and Printing
Production Director: Gerald Hughes
Production: Ruth Arthur, Neil Randles, Paul Randles,
Janine Seddon, Karen Staff

THE PHOTOGRAPHER

Neil Sutherland has more than 25 years experience in a wide range of
photographic fields, including still-life, portraiture, reportage, natural history,
cookery, landscape and travel. His work has been published in countless books
and magazines throughout the world.

Contributors

Peter Blackburne-Maze, Carol Gubler, John Feltwell, Nicholas Hall,
Jenny Hendy, Ann James, Yvonne Rees and Rosemary Titterington.

Half-title page: Tulipa 'West Point' and Myosotis alpestris in a classic clay pot.
*Title page: A barrel water feature and a summer display in a manger basket
dominated by petunias, geraniums, impatiens and ageratum.*
Left: A seaside collection of salt-tolerant plants in tones of silver, green and gray.
Right: A romantic wall basket of tuberous-rooted and bedding begonias.

CONTENTS
PART ONE: GARDENING IN CONTAINERS

Below: *Chimney pots make striking containers of different heights.*

Above: A plastic cauldron overflows with flowering plants.

Below: A sink garden of alpines and dwarf conifers.

CONTENTS
PART TWO: HANGING BASKETS AND WINDOWBOXES

Above: A trug filled with New Guinea hybrid Impatiens.

Above: Stencilling designs is easy and effective.

Below: A spring display of tulips, polyanthus, bellis daisies and violas.

Part One

GARDENING IN CONTAINERS

Gardening in containers is immensely exhilarating. Not only does it allow you to make the most of the space and time you have to spare, but as the variety of containers and suitable plants increases, it also opens up an exciting new range of creative possibilities bounded only by your imagination.

This first part of this book focuses on gardening in a wide range of containers, from tubs and barrels to troughs and growing bags. After looking at the style and suitability of a selection of containers, attention turns to growing climbing plants in tubs and troughs, with clematis, honeysuckles and climbing potatoes as the featured plants. Clematis, particularly, are great subjects for growing in tubs and once in full bloom they make wonderful centerpieces on a patio or porch. Fuchsias are also adaptable and elegant plants that can be shaped and presented in containers to great effect. The topics featured here include how to grow fuchsias around frames and hoops, how to trim plants to bonsai proportions and ideas for displaying fuchsias in novel containers. Novelty continues as the theme in a series of suggestions for presenting flowering plants in buckets, boots and chimney pots.

Containers can be used to create complete garden features in miniature, such as 'ponds' and rockeries, and play host to a succession of plants throughout the year, from spring bulbs to winter heathers. They can also support a surprising range of fruits, vegetables and herbs. All these themes are explored in this part of the book, complete with practical demonstrations that will inspire as well as inform you.

Left: Tulips and grape hyacinths in terracotta. ***Right:*** *A winter display of skimmia, primroses and variegated ivy.*

15

A selection of containers

Choosing the most suitable containers is as important as selecting the right plants. Stylish containers can help to establish the character of the garden, and so it is worth buying them with care. Matching sets of attractive, good-quality containers made of frostproof terracotta or painted and glazed ceramics, for example, can provide striking features in the garden. Although initially expensive, these will last for many years and look much better than cheap plastic containers. Reconstituted stone tubs, available in warm color tones, are also elegant and reassuringly stable in exposed sites. For the natural look, wooden barrels and troughs are hard to beat and you can make your own planters from wood with a little care and dedication. The plastic containers that mimic the finish of terracotta pots are particularly effective and superb value for money. You can even paint them to simulate the surface texture of older natural pots. Hanging baskets, wall pots and windowboxes are available in an equally wide range of materials and finishes.

Pieris forestii

Traditional oak barrel

Textured pot made from reconstituted paper

Mediterranean style terracotta pot

Reconstituted stone octagonal tub

Terracotta effect plastic pot

Wooden trough

Small terracotta pot cover with potted double primroses

Oriental ceramic pot

Classic-style square terracotta pot

Traditional wire basket with a liner made of reconstituted paper. Note the 'push-out' panels for planting through the sides.

Hanging pot with built-in drip tray

Large traditional terracotta pot. Being porous, terracotta pots dry out quickly.

Plastic self-watering hanging basket

Plastic self-watering wall planter

Terracotta wall planter

Natural sphagnum moss. This water-retentive material is traditionally used to line baskets. There are many modern alternatives.

Coco fiber basket liner

Metal 'hayrack' wall planter (needs a liner)

Coco-moss (natural coco fiber dyed green)

17

Planting clematis in a tub

4 With the plant in position, you can begin to set up the first part of the pyramid trellis. Ease it in carefully at the back of the tub, working the legs into the container without disturbing the plant.

Clematis are great subjects for displaying in tubs and once in full bloom they make a wonderful centerpiece on a patio or porch. Although pots and tubs are available in a wide range of different shapes and sizes, it is fun to use white tubs, since these have a very refreshing look. The great advantage of white is that it is distinctive and so easily coordinated with the rest of your garden furniture. The square tub - or Versailles tub - is a throwback to the grand tubs that once contained oranges and bougainvillea. Every year they were hauled in and out of the orangeries according to the seasons. Today's humble version may follow tradition and be made of wood or be a plastic simulation. Being small, it is much more versatile for the modern garden and, charged with its colorful clematis, can be moved around the garden or patio for instant effect. Choosing the right sort of clematis for the tub is very much a matter of individual choice. It might depend on your color scheme or it might reflect some particular clematis that you are attracted to, perhaps one of the large-flowered varieties with a compact growth habit. These are the most suitable for a small tub and trellis as shown on these pages, and the pink *Clematis* 'Hagley Hybrid' meets all these criteria. Once the clematis has become established on its support, trim it regularly if you want the trellis and clematis to feature as a little vignette of color on the patio. However, if you want a vigorous plant to continue climbing, you can allow it to form a substantial plant up a wall or as a bower.

1 Fill the bottom third of the tub with a proprietory potting mixture that contains a balance of peat, grit, sand and possibly fertilizer. Make a hole in the mixture to accept the rootball.

Stand the pot in a bucket of water to soak the roots before planting.

2 Carefully remove the plant from its pot. Hold onto the cane, as the stem might break if it falls away. Ease the clematis with its cane into the tub.

3 Add potting mix to within about 2in(5cm) of the top of the tub and firm it down. About 2in(5cm) of the stem should be covered with the soil.

Clematis 'Hagley Hybrid'

5 *Fit the next two sections of the pillar opposite each other and then work the legs into the potting mix, taking care not to damage the rootball. Follow the instructions.*

6 *Tie in any pieces of floppy vegetation to the trellis at regular intervals so that they are arranged as you wish, and to keep them away from the final stages of construction.*

7 *Ease in the final support without disturbing either the rest of it or the delicate stems or flower buds.*

Clematis for containers

'Bees Jubilee'
'Comtesse de Bouchaud'
'Edith'
'H.F. Young'
'Hagley Hybrid'
'Horn of Plenty'
'Lady Londesborough'
'Lady Northcliffe'
'Lasurstern'
'Miss Bateman'
'Mrs. N. Thompson'
'Nelly Moser'
'Souvenir de Capitaine Thuilleaux'

8 *As a finishing touch to the feature, put the white cap in place over the tapered ends of the wood. This secures them all in a pyramid shape.*

9 *Be sure to water the container profusely every day to ensure that the clematis becomes well established. Do not let it dry out at any stage.*

1 *Place your container in position. Put in a layer of crocks or stones to improve the drainage and fill it with a good-quality, well-balanced potting mixture. Do not use garden soil.*

A support is essential for the clematis to climb up.

Clematis in a wooden trough

Few gardeners realize the value of clematis as a container-grown plant, but in fact they are remarkably versatile, for a space in the border, as a patio plant, to provide welcome color early in the year or for a conservatory or cold greenhouse. There may be occasions when you would like to grow a clematis against a wall, but there is no border in which to plant it. A suitable container will answer this problem. Here we have used a wooden trough with an integral support, but you can use any suitable container and support system. You can grow a clematis like this in most locations and even move it when decoration or repairs are necessary. As long as it is not too heavy, you could use a container to disguise drain covers or unsightly areas to which you need access. Wooden containers tend to weather with age and eventually rot unless you protect them. The most effective and safest way is to paint them with an acrylic-based product, available in a wide range of colors and harmless to plants. With hardwood containers, just brush them with a little teak oil from time to

This plant support consists of thin strips of wood pulled across and interlocked under tension.

time to keep them fresh. Depending on the size of container, you can plant more than one clematis in it or fill the base with other plants. Montanas and the vigorous species do not do so well in containers as they soon outgrow their pot. The best choices are the large-flowered mid-season varieties with their stunning blooms, the smaller species, such as *C. alpina* and *C. florida*, and some of the more tender, early flowering types, such as *C. forsteri* and *C. armandii*. These last two will do well in a greenhouse, where you can appreciate their scent, even on the coldest days.

2 *Gently lower the clematis into place, with a few buds below the surface, and firm well in. Make sure there are no air gaps around the roots.*

6 *After a few weeks, begin feeding the plants with tomato fertilizer to ensure that the clematis gives a good display of flowers through the summer.*

4 Gently arrange the clematis shoots around the supports so that they eventually cover as much of them as possible. Loosely secure the shoots, using paper-covered wire plant ties.

5 Water the trough well in at this stage and continue to do so throughout the summer. Wooden, stone and terracotta pots may require more watering than plastic ones.

Continue training your clematis as it grows, taking care not to bruise the stems.

Hostas are particularly attractive to slugs, so place a few slug pellets around the base of each plant to prevent their very large leaves from being damaged.

3 In this trough, we have used hostas to fill the space around the base of the plant. They make a fine contrast with the clematis and grow exceptionally well in shade, but do require plenty of water to succeed.

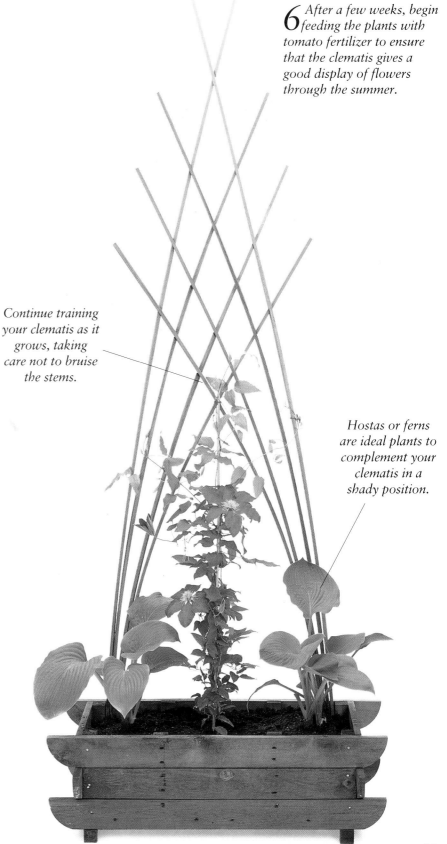

Hostas or ferns are ideal plants to complement your clematis in a shady position.

Clematis in a large patio container

This sort of container and its supports were designed primarily for growing runner beans, but it is an admirable means of displaying clematis on the patio. Because of its width, this container holds adequate potting mixture not only for the clematis, but also for a few bedding plants at the base. Here we have used *Begonia semperflorens,* but you could plant any low-growing annual. Alternatively, some of the Mediterranean plants with silver leaves will also thrive at the base of a clematis. Why not try some of the artemisias, such as *Artemisia frigida,* perhaps with some spring crocus underplanted to start the display? When selecting the clematis, avoid the vigorous growing varieties and use the more compact types, such as 'Lady Northcliffe' and 'Comtesse de Bouchaud', as here. The flowering periods of these two varieties flower overlap, which extends the period of interest of the container, and they require different pruning strategies. 'Lady Northcliffe' needs a light prune and 'Comtesse de Bouchaud', a hard prune, but the nature of the supports allows you to do this with ease. Choose your plants carefully; success will depend on the relation of the plants to their location. Remember that the container is open to the weather on all sides and that clematis with very large flowers may well be damaged by any strong summer winds. Finally, bear in mind that a large container complete with potting mixture is heavy, so put the container in its final position before planting.

There are various methods of training clematis. If the plant is growing in a tub against a wall or fence, you could choose a plastic or wooden system available from garden centers. Alternatively, you could make a dome of chicken wire over the container for the clematis to grow through, creating the impression of a potful of flowers. If you choose this method, start with a small plant or cut back a larger plant fairly hard. Another way is to train the clematis plants to spiral around five or six canes. The result is a stunning column of flowers.

1 Choose a potting mixture that will sustain your plants for several years. Clematis grow best in moist, well-drained, fertile soil, and need a cool root run.

2 Fill the container to within 1in(2.5cm) of the top to allow you to give the plants all the water and feed they require. You can always add more mixture later on if necessary.

3 Gently place the clematis into the container close to the supports. Make sure the rootball is not damaged and that some buds will be below soil level.

4 The simplest and least noticeable way of tying your clematis to the support is with paper-covered wire ties. Do not twist these too tight, as you can easily bruise the soft stems.

5 Once the clematis are secured, fill the remaining space with plants of your choice, ensuring that both they and the clematis are firmed in well.

6 Water the plants in until some water escapes from the base of the container. If the potting mix is well balanced, overwatering is not a problem.

7 Continue to water well while the plants establish themselves. They should not dry out. After two to three weeks, feed them with a tomato fertilizer.

8 After about two months, all your efforts will be rewarded with a magnificent show of flowers that will continue to give pleasure throughout the summer.

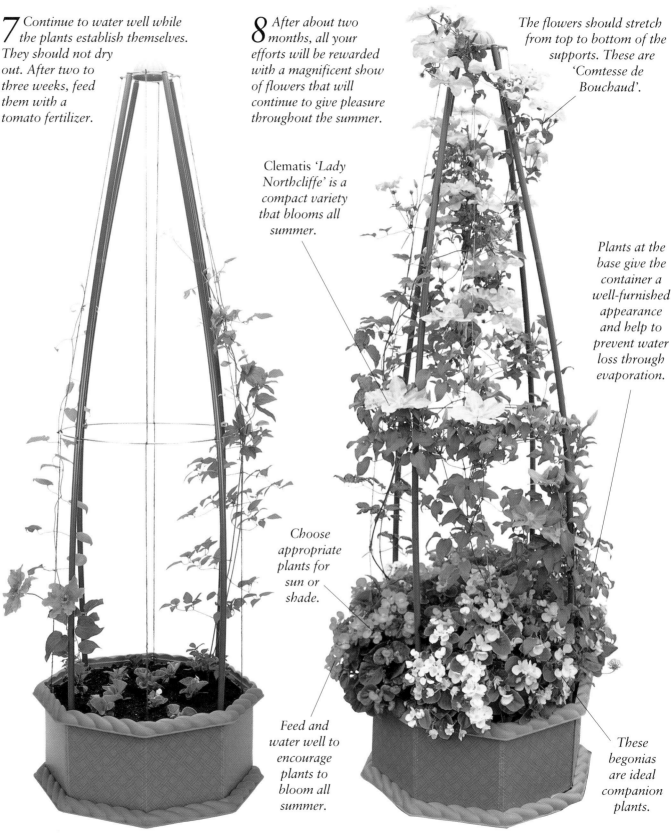

The flowers should stretch from top to bottom of the supports. These are 'Comtesse de Bouchaud'.

Clematis 'Lady Northcliffe' is a compact variety that blooms all summer.

Plants at the base give the container a well-furnished appearance and help to prevent water loss through evaporation.

Choose appropriate plants for sun or shade.

Feed and water well to encourage plants to bloom all summer.

These begonias are ideal companion plants.

Honeysuckle planted in a tub

Honeysuckles are universal favorites and there are many different species and cultivars to choose from. They can be grown in hedgerows, up trees, as pillars or as specimens in a tub with a trellis support. They are energetic stem climbers, have spectacular flowers and can fill the evening air with evocative scents. So which do you choose? There is a good chance that your native honeysuckle will perform the best in your area, but there are many others, such as *Lonicera periclymenum* or *L. etrusca* that you can grow as species of honeysuckles. Other good performers include *L.* x *americana*, 'Gold Flame' and the favorite, 'Graham Thomas' featured here. Honeysuckles can contribute to many yellow and green themes in the garden, whether they are grown in pots or not. You might consider Japanese honeysuckle, *Lonicera japonica* 'Aureoreticulata', or the yellow trumpet honeysuckle *L. sempervirens f. sulphurea*. In hotter areas with a typical Mediterranean climate, the Burmese honeysuckle, *Lonicera hildebrandtiana*, can look staggering with its 7in (18cm)-long yellow-orange giant flowers. This powerful climber is ideal for growing on pergolas, where it will relish the sunny conditions.

1 Fill the tub with a suitable potting mixture and make a hole in the center large enough for the rootball to fit with ease, allowing about 2in(5cm) of soil below the roots.

2 Tap the nursery plant out of its pot, together with its cane, and place the rootball into the hole, taking care not to lose too much of the soil adhering to the roots. Firm it in well.

3 Add more potting mixture around the plant. Distribute the mixture evenly in the box and level it off to within 2in(5cm) of the top of the pot to allow space for watering.

5 Use soft string to tie individual climbing stems to the trellis, taking care not to damage any of the delicate stems. Tie the knots loosely.

6 Also use string to tie the cane to the trellis. Again, take care not to crush or damage the climbing stems of the plant.

4 Gently firm in the soil around the plant to eliminate air gaps, which would prevent the roots developing. Add more potting mix if necessary, but leave a space at the top.

7 Give the honeysuckle a generous watering to ensure that it gets off to a good start. Water it every day for ten days so that it becomes established and do not allow it to dry out after that.

Planting a climbing potato

Climbing potatoes make exciting subjects in pots or tubs for their flowers and foliage and are fun to grow. They twine with their stems, but usually need a little support by being tied to trellis. It is best to choose a fairly large tub and to buy a well-grown nursery plant, such as the *Solanum jasminoides*, or potato vine, a native of Brazil. The white form, *Solanum jasminoides* 'Album', is featured on these pages. Climbing potatoes are best situated out of direct drafts and in a spot where they receive plenty of sun. There are other species that enjoy long hot summers, so where the climate is suitable try the erect blue potato tree, *Solanum rantonnetii*. This evergreen shrub bears deep purple flowers through the summer months and although not strictly a climber, can be trained to cover a warm, sheltered wall.

1 *Fill the pot to within about 4in (10cm) of the top with soil-based potting mixture. Trowel out sufficient soil to make a hole large enough to accommodate the rootball.*

2 *Soak the potted plant in water and allow it to drain. Tap it out of its pot, with its cane, and insert it into the soil so that the stem is covered by about 2in(5cm) of soil. Firm the plant in with your knuckles.*

3 *Having firmed down all round the edges of the planted climber, top up the tub with more potting mix to within about 2in(5cm) of the top of the pot. Firm down lightly once more.*

4 Cut off some of the nursery ties, especially if they are too tight and restricting plant growth, but take care as you release the plant. Separate the various climbing stems.

5 You will need a few ties to attach the climbing stems to the trellis. Twist ties are the easiest to use, as they can be quickly put in place, adjusted or moved as the plant grows.

Tie in new growth as necessary. This Solanum jasminoides 'Album' can grow up to 20ft(6m).

6 Give the plant a good watering to encourage it to grow in the best possible conditions. Water it every day for about ten days and then check it regularly to make sure that it does not dry out.

7 The green trellis is a good contrast against the white wall and shows off the plant to advantage.

Frames and hoops

Fuchsia growing should be fun and it is not always important that the plants are grown in conventional shapes. There are times when it is worthwhile experimenting. Many cultivars have a very supple growth that you can bring under control with a little training. The advantage of growing fuchsias around wire or plastic shapes is that you do not have to worry about stopping times - as the plant grows, it flowers! There are several points to bear in mind. Firstly, if you are using wire, try to use a plastic-coated kind, otherwise the heat from the wire can burn the plants during the summer months. Secondly, think about the cultivar that you are choosing. If you want a small shape, use a small-flowered type, as a large flower would look totally out of proportion. It is not always necessary to use the most floriferous cultivars, as continually tying or bending in the young growth will enhance any floral display simply because the flowers are so much closer together. This applies particularly to the encliandras; with their extremely small flowers they can look sparse in other circumstances. Using more than one plant in the pot can make growing a three-dimensional structure much easier.
Finally, do not be discouraged if you do not achieve the expected result first time; a little perseverance will certainly pay off!

Decorative shapes

Making shapes is as simple as bending the wire. As long as the angles are not too extreme, fuchsias will accommodate to a wide range of forms. Why not try your house number or your initials? All it needs are nimble fingers and a degree of patience. Be imaginative and adventurous!

Right: F. hidalgensis, *with its attractive, small white flowers, has been used to form this globe.*

Far right: *A spiral is easy to make using the same species, one of the most supple for this purpose.*

Cultivars for growing into shapes

F. hidalgensis, F. hemsleyana, *La Campanella, Lottie Hobbie, Mrs. Lovell Swisher, Mrs. Popple, Neapolitan, Northway, Pink Rain, String of Pearls, Topper, Whiteknights Pearl*

Use a plastic frame or plastic-covered wire to avoid the risk of scorching growth in hot weather.

1 *Fuchsias can easily be trained into a shape while they are young and supple, so start at this stage. Add the wire before the plant has grown too large, shaping it to the required size and shape.*

2 *Use soft ties that will not damage the tender young growth. Add more ties every few days to ensure that the fuchsia is closely molded to the wire shape while the growth is still supple. Fuchsias can grow quickly!*

Coping with large shaped fuchsias

Take care when potting on fuchsias that have been grown in elaborate shapes. You may need a helper to balance and support the frame. Large hoops are a little flimsy until they have become established, so do not leave them in a windy position. Be sure to give these pots a full half turn to ensure that they grow evenly; a quarter turn is not enough. For the best results, tie in the growth every two or three days. This ensures that the shape remains neat.

3 *The plants need no stopping, because they flower as they grow. It is important to maintain a regular feeding program to ensure fine healthy growth at all times.*

4 *Eventually the circle is complete and Whiteknights Pearl is beginning to come into flower. Choose a cultivar with flowers in proportion to the size of the shape. A strong grower is also useful.*

Fuchsias in novel containers

Let your imagination run riot when considering the containers in which your fuchsias will look good growing and flowering. They do not have to be on a grand scale, but make sure they are in proportion to the size of the plant and the flowers. Small plants in small containers can be great fun. Look for containers with some kind of drainage. If there is none, then it may be possible to make holes in the base, but only if you do not want to use it for anything else afterwards! If drainage remains poor, water very carefully, giving your plants just the merest drop as necessary. A terracotta container with poor drainage is not such a problem as it is porous and water can seep out of the sides, thus reducing the potential problems. Try matching fuchsia names with containers; for example, Trumpeter in a trumpet, Peppermint Stick in a candy jar. Or why not match the size and shape of the plant to the style of the container?

If possible, put the plant in your chosen container long before it is in flower so that the stress of the change does not cause it to drop flowers and buds. If it has to be a last-minute enterprise, keep the plant in a cool, shady spot for as long as possible to reduce the stress and allow it to recover from the change.

Points to watch

Take care when watering novelty containers, as many have poor drainage or none at all. Water them sparingly and do not forget to feed them. Try to find containers that are in proportion to the size of the flowers and growth habit of the plant; a small plant in a large pot (or vice-versa) can look very strange.

With its slightly trailing growth, Autumnale (Burning Bush), makes an ideal plant for this small display. As the plants are in ordinary pots on saucers it is easy to change the plants.

30

A watering can is an ideal container, provided you make plenty of drainage holes in the base. Do not put it in full sun for long, as the heat could cause the roots to scorch. Wassernymph (Waternymph) seems an ideal choice.

Dancing Flame makes a fine display trailing over a terracotta cauldron. The plant can lose moisture through the porous pot, as well as via the drainage holes.

A plant in a shoe is always a talking point. Push the potting mix very gently to the extremities, so that the roots can spread around. Olive Smith, a small, single-flowered cultivar, seems to be thriving.

A small kettle with a large plant; this one is Superstar. Take care when planting around the handle. Gently maneuver the branches around it to achieve the desired effect.

Drainage can be a major problem in a glazed pottery teapot with no holes. Water very carefully, giving only small quantities as and when the plant and potting mixture become dry.

1 *Remove as much soil and as many fibrous roots as possible from the plant you have chosen to train, so that it will fit into the shallow bonsai container.*

Fuchsias as bonsai

Growing fuchsias as bonsai subjects is as much of a challenge as creating large structures. However, fuchsias are more than happy to be root-pruned and this makes them ideal candidates for bonsai. The most important thing is to choose the right varieties of fuchsia to grow, as the proportion of the plant to the container and the fuchsia's general growth pattern are clearly vital considerations. Large flowers on a small plant in a small pot would look quite wrong. You will have to rethink some basic gardening principles, too. For example, a plant with a balanced shape is no longer the aim. Have a look at any less than perfect plants and you may well find a potential bonsai. Plants with a woody stem in their second year are ideal candidates, and as with any other bonsai, you can use wire to help create a shape. Judicious pruning and positioning in the pot make the plant look more authentic.

Never give bonsai fuchsia a high-nitrogen feed; a weak solution of a balanced feed is best. Keep the plants in a shady position to prevent them drying out. Gentle watering with a fine spray will gradually bring the top roots to the surface and expose them, and you can further enhance the bonsai effect by adding a little moss. Bonsai fuchsias can remain in the same container for many years. Give them an annual root prune and add some fresh potting mixture at the same time. They will give you much pleasure in this unusual form.

2 *If there are any larger roots that would be difficult to fit into a shallow pot, carefully trim these with secateurs. Do not worry - your plant will survive.*

3 *Choose the best position for planting your fuchsia in its pot. It need not be symmetrical, but should create a pleasing, bonsai-like appearance.*

4 *Gently trickle more soil into the tiny gaps around the roots. A small spoon is ideal for this. Do not press the soil down; it will find its own level.*

Put the moss gently in position. It will soon regrow.

5 For a final bonsai touch, add a small piece of moss around the main stem. Put it in place and shape it as necessary. This piece came from the surface of an old fuchsia.

6 This is a good opportunity to trim branches and carry out any stopping required to shape the plant. To achieve an authentic bonsai shape, wire soft branches into 'windswept' positions.

7 Once you are happy with the plant, give it a little water and place it in a cool, shady spot. Leave it in this stress-free environment for up to a week and water it as necessary.

Suitable fuchsias to grow as bonsai

Where possible, try to look for plants with small flowers and a small growth habit, as they will look ideal as a bonsai. With their small leaves and delicate flowers, encliandras are good subjects, and so are the dwarf-growing hardies, such as Tom Thumb and Lady Thumb. Try foliage fuchsias as well. Always be prepared to experiment.

A three-year-old Pumilla fuchsia.

David, an old, low-growing hardy, is an excellent choice.

To achieve this sort of shape, bend wire gently around a young and supple stem.

33

Unusual containers

Any number of unusual and amusing bygones have been pressed into service as plant containers in the cottage garden, from boots and buckets to chimney pots and saucepans. Saucepans and buckets are a good shape, as they have relatively straight sides; if you intend to plant directly into them, remember to drill drainage holes in the base, but it is easier simply to stand a plant pot raised on a layer of shingle inside. However enticing, any shape that curves in too acutely at the top, such as a kettle, makes a poor container. Not only is the hole too small to accept a decent-sized flowerpot, but it is also difficult to give the plant sufficient water once its roots have spread inside.

The popularity of old kitchen sinks as containers for miniature alpine or Japanese gardens remains undiminished and even though the original stone sinks are no longer available, you can make an acceptable substitute by giving a more recent white-glazed sink a covering of hypertufa. Bind together equal parts of sand, cement and peat with water. Apply a coat of adhesive over the sink and after it has dried, press the mixture on with your hands. Leave the container to dry thoroughly before planting it up.

Traditional galvanized buckets are still produced and make good planters. You can give them an attractive matt black appearance by applying a coat of blackboard paint, which has the advantage of drying very quickly.

1 *Apply the black paint evenly, retouching it where necessary after it has dried. Blackboard paint will dry in less than an hour.*

2 *Drill a hanging hole in the back. Support the bucket on end, with the straining cone downwards, and half fill it with garden soil.*

3 *Leave the plants in pots until they have grown on to ensure that they have enough light and water. Replant into the bucket, with potting mix, later.*

Pelargonium 'Salmon Queen' (ivy-leaved trailing geranium)

Above: Old leather boots acquire a new lease of life as home to a pretty mix of Ajuga 'Burgundy Glow' and Viola 'Purple Duet'.

Below: California poppies, Eschscholzia californica, make a stunning feature blooming in an old iron cooking pot on the patio.

4 Arrange the pots around the 'upper' half of the bucket, supporting the top pot if necessary to keep it well forward. Water well.

5 Hang the bucket on a screw or nail - remembering to hang the handle downwards - and keep it well-watered. Deadhead flowers regularly.

Pansies in a metal bucket

1 Here, the bucket is left unpainted and used as a pot holder. Put a layer of shingle on the base of the bucket to raise the base of the pot and improve drainage.

2 Choose a flowerpot with a diameter that fits comfortably inside the bucket. Plant it up with a selection of suitable plants and stand it on the bed of shingle.

3 The cheerful little viola 'Jackanapes', bred by Gertrude Jekyll, mixes well with a pansy of the same color combination.

Pots of plants

Pot plants are the gardener's ever-present help in time of need, whether it is to conceal and transform an eyesore into a stunning focal point, plump up a tired flower bed, or bring impact to a dull area. They also provide an opportunity for growing specimens unsuited to your conditions; because their requirements are individually catered for, you can grow virtually anything you wish. In general, pots in a group should be of the same color and material - terracotta for example - and fairly plain. You can, of course, paint an assortment of pots to achieve a matching appearance. Small pots and bowls work effectively for dot plants, but where pots are grouped together use fewer and larger containers, otherwise the result is an untidy and unsatisfactory muddle. Remember that the smaller the pot the faster it dries out. At the top end of the market are the exquisite handmade Greek pithoi, too beautiful in themselves to need plants in them. Reproduction period urns and tubs, better used alone or as a pair, lend themselves to foliage plants, such as hostas, or the felted silver or soft lime leaves of *Helichrysum petiolatum*, perhaps planted with single blue petunias or white trailing pelargoniums. Dot plants are fun; try experimenting with some of the smaller perennials, such as *Heuchera*, or the slow, clump-forming grasses and ferns. Give larger pots some protection from frost by raising them on small clay feet. However, if not guaranteed frostproof, there is no certainty that they will not shatter unless made of plastic.

Plants for pots 12in (30cm) and more

Pieris, *azalea and dwarf* Rhododendron. *Plant these in ericaceous potting mixture and keep in partial shade.*

Ferns, grasses and hostas. Keep them moist and in light shade.

Agapanthus, *species gladioli,* Nerine *and species tulips. These bulbs require sharp drainage and a sunny site.*

Argyranthemum '*Jamaica Primrose*', *bay trees,* Bidens aurea, Chaenomeles '*Simonii*', Felicia amelloides *and* Osteospermum *need sun.*

1 Select a good-sized pot and place a few pieces of broken clay pot or pebbles in the base to prevent the drainage hole getting blocked.

2 Half-fill the pot with good-quality potting mixture. If you have chosen really acid-loving lilies, be sure to plant them in an ericaceous mix.

3 Slide your fingers between the stems to support the plant without damage. Upend the pot and tap the base to shake the root free safely.

Asiatic hybrids are short, easy and lime-tolerant. Buy bulbs directly from growers.

Left: *A group of plants in generously proportioned terracotta pots makes up the heaped bank of color on the corner of this terrace where there is no space for a flower bed.*

4 *Supporting the roots with both hands, place the plant gently on the potting mixture. Follow the same procedure for the other lilies, spacing them equally.*

'Denia Pixie'

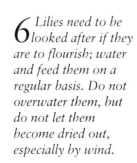

'Buff Pixie'

'Orange Pixie'

5 *Carefully fill up the spaces between the stems with potting mixture. Firm it gently with your fingers and water the container. If any depressions appear, fill them with more potting mixture.*

6 *Lilies need to be looked after if they are to flourish; water and feed them on a regular basis. Do not overwater them, but do not let them become dried out, especially by wind.*

Chimney pots as planters

Chimney pots, both old and new, make a striking display when used in groups of varying styles and height. When planting a tall container of this sort, it is better to find a plastic plant pot (or bucket) large enough to lodge in the top. If you fill the chimney itself with soil, it will become too dry and compacted to support a healthy plant - and also immovable. Look at your chimney pot both ways up before deciding how to use it; many, especially the tall ones, are a better shape upside-down and more effective planted this way, because being wider at the base, they will hold a larger pot. The height of the chimney will dictate the type of plants to grow in it; the tallest ones look better with plants that flow out and down, such as ivy or trailing geraniums. There are also plenty of tender perennials to choose from. Short, stubby little pots look equally good with erect, bushy or trailing plants, such as *Phormium*, grasses, *Hosta* and *Helianthemum*.

It is often a great help to be able to raise a group of plants in, or at the back of, the flower bed for those times when there is a gap in the flowering succession, or to keep it going when it is past its best. With their narrow, straight lines, the tall chimney pots are excellent used in this way.

1 In this instance, the chimney pot has been reversed. Choose a flowerpot with a suitable diameter to lodge inside the rim.

A hosta in a short chimney pot

1 Because this is only a short pot - just 12in (30cm) high - it does not need to be lined with a flowerpot before you start planting it up.

2 Two-thirds fill with a mixture of good-quality soil and potting mixture or potting mixture alone.

2 Put a few broken crocks in the bottom of the flowerpot to improve drainage, and add potting mixture until it is two-thirds full.

3 Place the first plant well over to one side of the pot, so that it leans outwards a little. Cover the roots with a small amount of potting mixture.

The gracefully drooping stems of Osteospermum 'Sunny Girl', 'Sunny Boy' and 'Langtrees' are perfect for a tall pot or urn.

The scarlet Pelargonium 'Mars' in a modern 'cannon-head' 18in(45cm) pot.

Golden Helichrysum petiolatum will spread out and down to balance Pelargonium 'Knaufs Bonfire' and salmon-pink Geranium 'Rokoko'.

Hosta fortunei aureomarginata has fragrant spikes of lavender flowers in summer. Keep it moist and cool.

3 *Gently tease out and separate the roots and then place the plant in the pot. Water it in, fill up with potting mix and water again.*

4 *Position the remaining plants around the pot in the same way. Generously fill the spaces between them with potting mixture, firm down and water well.*

Above: *With their clean lines and architectural presence, chimney pots make ideal plant holders used together or individually for height and emphasis.*

Creeping Jenny Lysimachia nummularia 'Aurea' in a small pot. Keep it out of strong sun and wind or it will scorch.

39

Creating a water feature in a barrel

If you would really like a pond feature, but have no room in the garden or on the patio, or if excavations and major building work are impractical, you can always set up a miniature pool in a pot, tub or other suitable container. Providing they are scaled down, you can have all the features you set your heart on; water lilies, marginal plants, fish and even a tiny, sparkling fountain. The finished tub can be a real focal point and provide hours of pleasure for very little outlay in terms of time and money, as well as space. Any waterproof container is suitable, from a large cut-down barrel to a small terracotta or plastic patio pot. The only real proviso is that the chosen container has not been treated with any poisonous or fungicidal chemicals that might damage plants and fish. Some garden centers sell tub kits that come complete with everything you need, even a selection of plants, to be assembled at home. Alternatively, buy a ready-made bubble fountain in a stone or terracotta container, with plants and pebbles installed for an instant moving water feature.

2 Since the wooden barrel is not waterproof, the first task is to line it. Use a large piece of proper pond liner and push it firmly down inside.

3 Trim off some of the excess at this stage, but leave plenty around the edges to allow for it to settle down further as you add water and bricks.

1 These are the ingredients to make a stunning water feature in a tub. It is a good idea to set out what you plan to include in the final display before you start work. This also gives you the chance to see whether the elements will look good together.

Make sure this tube is firmly pushed into the pump.

4 Put the pump in now. This is a small, mains-powered model ideally suited to the size of the display. Place it on a brick for stability and to bring it up to the correct height.

5 Place a layer of bricks around the inside of the barrel. These will provide platforms to support the plant pots and stones. Use hard bricks sold for paving; they are more durable in water.

6 Add some cobbles to fill in the spaces between the bricks. These will help to stabilize the piles of bricks and will also stop the pump moving around once the feature is operating.

7 Add a top layer of paving bricks. These will support the large stones and plant pots of the final display. Build the bricks up in stable patterns to avoid problems later on.

8 Now add the large stones that will form the visible part of the feature. Rounded boulders such as these not only look attractive but will also stand continuous immersion in water.

9 Add water until it reaches the base of the boulders. This will leave enough expansion room to add the plants and final stones.

Planting up the barrel

Here we show how to plant up the barrel prepared on pages 40-41. Of course, all kinds of troughs, pots, tubs and barrels are suitable for planting up in this way. Just make sure that they are painted inside with a sealant or lined with butyl rubber or plastic pond liner to ensure that they are watertight. Do remember that once filled with water, a few plants and any other water features you may chose, such as an ornament or fountain, the tub or pot is going to be extremely heavy, so decide on its final position while it is empty and plant it up in situ. If you are going to have to move the feature, place the container on a low platform with lockable casters for mobility. A water feature in a tub makes an excellent focal point for a dull corner of the garden or patio, where it might be raised on such a platform or a few bricks for extra prominence. Alternatively, stand it on a bed of pebbles or gravel or surround it with large stones and pots of lush plants to reinforce the watery effect. To show the tub at its best, make sure you position it against a suitable backdrop, such as a wall, fence or plain greenery. Large pebbles or a wall behind are also useful for installing concealed spouts for moving water effects to enhance the feature.

1 If you want to neaten things up a bit at this stage you can trim off more of the liner. The weight of the water will have pushed the liner into its final position.

2 Now begin to add the plants. Since they will be immersed in water, you can choose from a wide range of marginal plants that thrive in these conditions. Pot them into the plastic mesh baskets that you use for the pond.

Smooth stones or boulders look best in small pools.

3 If the display has a definite front view, then plan the planting with this in mind. Adding this low growing water forget-me-not towards the front will work well with the tall water buttercup at the back of the barrel.

4 *Once the planting is complete, you can add more stones to fill in spaces that seem to 'appear'. Adding another boulder here creates a better display. Be careful not to dislodge the outlet pipe of the pump as you move heavy items around.*

5 *Add cobbles and pebbles to match the color range and shape of the boulders. This helps the feature to look more like the bank of a natural stream. By now the barrel is very heavy and you should be working on it in its final location in the garden setting.*

Lysimachia thyrsiflora

Ranunculus flammula

Iris versicolor *'Blue Light'*

Myosotis palustris

Epimedium x youngianum *'Roseum'* (Not a marginal but would look attractive close to the barrel.)

Primula veris (Not suitable for inside the barrel, but this bog garden plant thrives in damp soil.)

6 *This is the final display with a three-tier spray fountain head fitted to the pump. The edges of the liner have been trimmed neatly around the top of the barrel.*

7 *If you prefer a bell-shaped effect then fit the appropriate head. Be careful not to pull out the central tube of the pump when changing heads.*

A rockery in a trough

Few gardens today have room for a conventional rockery, but a miniature version in a container makes a most attractive feature on paving near a back door or seat. Team rockery-themed containers with gravel or cobbled paths, or tuck them into odd sunny corners around the garden. Stone sinks were once the traditional containers for alpines, but you can use virtually any sort of container, as long as it can withstand exposure to frost and has good drainage. Large terracotta pots, deep ceramic dishes and plastic troughs are all suitable. Check that there are plenty of holes in the base, and if not, drill more. Nurseries and garden centers offer a huge range of rockery plants, but vigorous spreading kinds will soon become a nuisance in a confined space, so restrict yourself to compact cushion- and bun-shaped plants. If you choose spreading plants such as aubretia, which make carpets of color, place them at the edge of the container so they can trail over the sides and make sure you can replace them easily with smaller plants when they outgrow their welcome. Since the majority of popular rock plants are spring-flowering, include plants with attractive, preferably evergreen, foliage to keep the display looking good all year round. You can also find ultra-dwarf trees such as *Betula nana*, to help create mini-landscapes.

1 Select a suitable container with several holes in the base. This one is actually made from styrofoam. Place 1in(2.5cm) of gravel in the bottom to improve the drainage.

2 Place the largest rock in position before filling the container with potting mixture. This way it is easier to move around, and will look more natural partly buried.

3 Fill the container almost to the rim with soil-based potting mixture; this can be mixed with a small amount of fine grit to improve drainage even more.

4 Add a couple of smaller rocks to complement the larger chunk. Again, partly bury them in the potting mixture for a more natural effect and to prevent them becoming dislodged.

Potted rockeries

Spring: *Trim back dead stems and sprinkle fresh gravel around plants. Feed with half-strength, general-purpose liquid feed when plants begin growing well and remove dead flowerheads.*
Summer: *Feed monthly as before and water the container well whenever the soil feels dry.*
Fall: *Remove any seedheads and sow seed straight away. Stop feeding; water only in dry spells.*
Winter: *Rock plants are at risk of rotting in winter, so ensure that containers are sheltered from excess rain and raised up on bricks, allowing surplus water to drain away quickly.*

5 *Choose a selection of rock plants with different shapes, flower colors and leaf textures. Stand the pots roughly in position while you plan where to plant each one.*

6 *Knock each plant out of its pot, and scoop out a hole in the potting mix large enough to take the roots comfortably. Avoid breaking up the rootball of the plant.*

7 *Topdress with a layer of fine grit, which helps prevent the necks of the plants rotting. Raise the container up on bricks to ensure good drainage.*

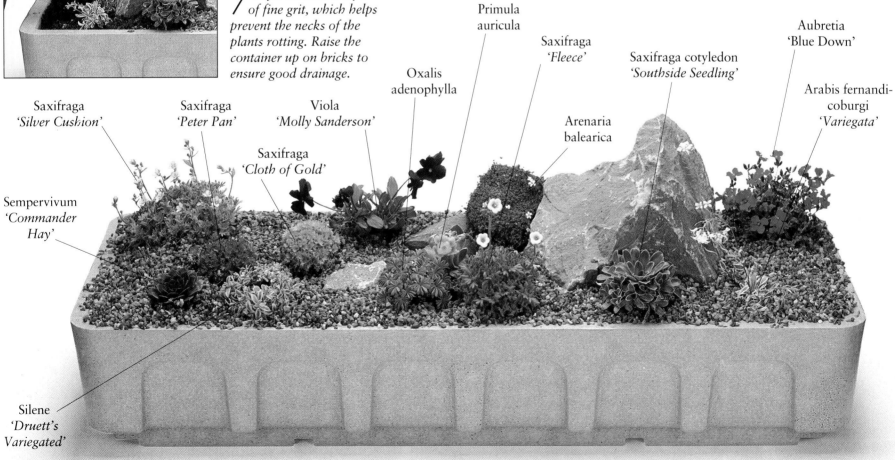

Primula auricula

Saxifraga 'Fleece'

Saxifraga cotyledon 'Southside Seedling'

Aubretia 'Blue Down'

Oxalis adenophylla

Arenaria balearica

Arabis fernandi-coburgi 'Variegata'

Saxifraga 'Silver Cushion'

Saxifraga 'Peter Pan'

Viola 'Molly Sanderson'

Saxifraga 'Cloth of Gold'

Sempervivum 'Commander Hay'

Silene 'Druett's Variegated'

A sink garden

With their sculptured shapes and dense foliage, compact, slow-growing conifers make a good year-round backdrop for seasonal flowering rock plants, which enjoy the same growing conditions. A sink garden will need regular attention. Watering is the most frequent chore; you can't assume natural rainfall will be sufficient. Feed every two weeks from spring to late summer or add a slow-release fertilizer to the potting mix before planting the container, and add a new supply each spring by making a few holes in the potting mix and putting the feed down them. After two or three years the potting mix will be exhausted and need replacing, and some of the plants will have become untidy or overgrown, so the sink garden is best dismantled and remade using fresh plants. You can then plant out the old ones onto a rock garden or raised bed.

1 Choose a mixture of plants that contrast well together in shape, texture and color while providing year-round interest. You will also need a bag of soil-based potting mixture.

2 Cover the large drainage holes in the bottom of the container with flat pieces of stone or broken pieces of clay flowerpot. Add a 1in(2.5cm) layer of coarse gravel to cover the base of the container evenly.

3 Now part fill the 'sink' with soil-based potting mixture, leaving enough room to take the plants when standing in their pots, plus a margin of about 0.5in (1.25cm) between the pot and the rim of the container.

4 Carefully position the largest plants; they will make the most impact on the finished arrangement. Knock the plants out of their pots and stand them in place; position a curving conifer so it leans towards the center of the container.

5 *Place the second conifer alongside and push both conifers as close to the back of the container as possible, since they will be the tallest plants and will form a background to the display.*

6 *Tuck rock plants into the gaps left between the conifers and the edge of the container; if necessary squeeze the rootballs slightly to flatten them to fit, but avoid damaging the roots.*

7 *Plants with a slightly trailing habit at the front of the container will cascade over the edge and soften the hard lines. Use plenty of plants so that the container looks full.*

8 *Add a little extra potting mix to fill any gaps between rootballs. After watering in, this extra mix will probably sink slightly, so top up any depressions with extra mixture later.*

Hedera helix 'Conglomerata'

Chamaecyparis pisifera 'Nana Aureovariegata'

Sempervivum 'Pruhonice'

Chamaecyparis pisifera 'Golden Nymph'

Sedum lydium

Arabis fernandi-coburgi 'Variegata'

Thymus 'Doone Valley'

Hypericum empetrifolium prostratum

47

Bulbs in a container

Containers are the ideal way of growing bulbs that need different conditions from those in the open garden; perhaps better drainage (some bulbs, such as tulips, rot easily in cold wet soil). And being portable, containers enable you to rearrange patio and doorstep displays for seasonal effect - try teaming a tub of flowering spring bulbs with all-year-round containers of evergreens or conifers. Pots of flowering bulbs are available in garden centers in spring; plunge them to the rims into tubs of old potting mix for an instant display. But it is much more satisfying to create displays with dry bulbs in fall and cheaper, too. Start with new containers and potting mixture or remove old summer bedding plants from existing containers; you can reuse the old soil, but loosen it first with a fork. Most popular spring bulbs are suitable for containers, but compact cultivars make a tighter group and are less likely to suffer broken stems in windy weather. It is best to plant each container with one type of bulb, but if you want to mix different kinds together, choose those that flower at the same time, otherwise the display will be spoiled by old foliage when the later ones come into bloom. Start liquid feeding regularly when the first buds appear.

Soil-based potting mix

Gritty sand

1 *Assemble a large clay pot, gritty sand, soil-based potting mix and your chosen bulbs. Cover the hole in the base of the pot with a broken 'crock'.*

2 *Scoop 1-2in(2.5-5cm) of gritty sand into the base of the pot to cover the crock. This provides extra drainage, which is beneficial in containers that are left out in winter.*

3 *Cover the grit with 1-2in(2.5-5cm) of potting mixture, so that the pot is roughly half-filled. Do not firm the mixture down at this stage - this is to allow bulbs to be pressed into it.*

A soil-based potting mixture is best for bulbs, as it retains less water than peat types.

Use clay pots for displays of bulbs, as they are porous.

4 *Press the bulbs gently into the potting mix. Put in as many as you can for a good display. Adjacent bulbs should not quite touch each other or the side of the pot. These are daffodils.*

5 Cover the daffodil bulbs, leaving only the tips showing. This allows a second tier of bulbs to be planted in the gaps without risk of damage.

6 Grape hyacinths flower at the same time as daffodils and have similar requirements, but plant them less deeply. Press the bulbs between the daffodils.

7 Trowel *more potting mix carefully over the grape hyacinth bulbs.* Fill the pot to within 1in(2.5cm) of the rim. Leave some space for watering.

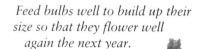

Lift the pot onto 'pot feet' to improve the drainage.

8 You can stand the pot out of the way until the bulbs are in flower, but usually it is more convenient to place it in its final flowering position at this stage. Water well.

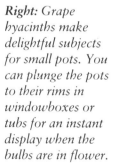

Left: Narcissi (daffodils) root early, so plant the bulbs as soon as they are available in late summer or early fall, especially if they are early-flowering kinds, such as 'February Gold'.

Feed bulbs well to build up their size so that they flower well again the next year.

Right: Grape hyacinths make delightful subjects for small pots. You can plunge the pots to their rims in windowboxes or tubs for an instant display when the bulbs are in flower.

Tuberous begonias in tubs

Tuberous begonias are very useful flowers all around the house and garden. Use them on windowsills, in sunrooms, porches or a greenhouse, and outdoors in containers or beds. There are various types: the normal, upright-growing, double-flowered plant in a range of colors; trailing begonias for hanging baskets; and cultivars with unusual flower forms, such as anemone-centered, semi-double or frilled-edged. The very large-flowered kinds are intended for exhibition and need greenhouse cultivation. In spring, you can buy dry, dormant begonia tubers, which are easy to grow. Established plants in pots are also available all summer. However, the cheapest way to acquire a good collection is to grow your own from seed. Sprinkle the dustlike seed thinly on the surface of finely sifted seed mixture, and cover the pot with plastic film. Stand the pot in a dish of tepid water until it is completely moist. Keep it in a warm place at a steady temperature and out of direct sunlight. When the seedlings are large enough, prick them out individually into a tray of similar seed mix, and cover them with a plastic propagator lid to retain humidity. Finally, pot the seedlings individually into small pots. Expect seed-raised plants to start flowering in their second year.

Tuberous begonias lose their stems and leaves in the fall; when they start yellowing in late summer, reduce the feed and water until the soil in the pots is quite dry. Store the pots in a dry, frost-free place for the winter, or empty the pots and store the dry tubers in paper bags in a drawer indoors.

Above: *To produce large blooms on a tuberous begonia, nip out the two tiny buds on either side of the main flower. This variety is called 'Pin Up'.*

1 *To avoid planting begonia tubers upside down, sit the dry corms convex side up in a dish of damp seed mixture on a warm windowsill.*

2 *When fat pink buds are visible in the dished surface of the corm, you can be certain it has started to grow and is the right way up, although no roots have appeared yet. This is the right stage for potting.*

3 *To plant the corm, loosely fill a 4 or 5in(10 or 13cm) diameter pot with potting mixture to within 0.5in(1.25cm) of the rim. The potting mixture can be either peat, coir or soil-based.*

Left: *A row of similar tuberous begonias makes an attractive semi-formal feature in a terracotta trough. The effect is of a cottage windowsill. Deadhead regularly to keep new buds coming all summer.*

Right: *Trailing tuberous begonias are good for hanging baskets, here seen growing with fuchsia, lobelia, busy lizzie and petunias. Trailing begonias need not be disbudded, as they naturally have many smaller flowers.*

5 *The end result: a well-grown begonia plant with perfect blooms the size of tea cups that make a stunning display in their container.*

Right: *Once the plant is coming into flower, you can transfer it to a larger container, such as this formal outdoor urn.*

4 *Press the base of the corm firmly into the center of the pot, leaving the very top of the corm just showing above the surface. Water; keep out of bright sun until growing well.*

1 *The secret of success when pairing plants and containers is to put everything together in a group before buying, so you can gauge the effect.*

Planting up a plastic cauldron

One of the things that makes container gardening fun is the way you can keep finding new combinations of pots and plants that work well together. Try out new kinds of plants that you find in garden centers and do not always go for the same species, color schemes or style. And experiment with different kinds of containers - even ones that perhaps look a little unlikely to start with. There is no need to spend a fortune. Cheap plastic containers can be made to look sensational, given the right sort of plants to bring out their hidden depths, and secondhand 'finds' in junk shops or rummage sales can be given a new lease of life with an unusual paint effect or simply by cleaning them up. If you cannot take an existing container to the nursery with you, try to find something similar in the shop and stand your basket of plants next to it to see how they look. Also look at the striking ready-planted containers that many garden centers set up, both to tempt people who prefer not to bother making up their own, but to give good ideas to those who do. If you grow your own plants from seed, you can judge the effect of various flowers and containers by cutting pictures from magazines and catalogs - that way, you can have all the fun of planning your summer displays in midwinter, in good time to send off your seed order.

2 *Almost fill the container to the rim with potting mixture and knock each plant in turn out of its pot. Avoid breaking the rootball.*

3 *Position the largest and most striking plant in the center of the container and fit the others around its roots in the remaining space.*

6 Use the shortest plants at the front of the display, encouraging them where possible to spill over the front of the container, thus softening the hard line of the edge.

Pelargonium

Striped single French marigolds

Calceolaria (new colorful outdoor strains, resembling those previously only available as indoor pot plants).

French marigolds

4 Group plants with different shaped flowers next to each other. Plant the palest species towards the front to add depth to the display.

5 Use a narrow trowel to tuck spare soil into the gaps between rootballs. When all the plants are in place, add 0.5in(1.25cm) of soil over the entire surface.

French marigolds

Mini outdoor 'Carnival' chrysanthemums

Mimulus

Winter-flowering tubs

All the plants suggested for winter hanging baskets (page 166) are equally suitable for containers. Being closer to ground level, tubs suffer less from the weather, so you can grow a wider range of plants, including winter-flowering heathers (page 56), Christmas rose *(Helleborus niger)*, early spring bulbs and any of the early spring bedding plants. It is also possible to use taller plants, such as evergreen shrubs, as the centerpiece of a floral display; variegated or colored kinds, such as euonymus and *Choisya ternata* 'Sundance', whipcord *Hebe* 'James Stirling' or dwarf conifers, are good. Plants bought straight from a garden center are ideal. Shrubs can remain in their new containers for a couple of years, but will fairly quickly fill them with root, preventing new bedding plants being put in to replace those that are over. So unless the plant is to become a solo specimen, repot it with new flowers into a larger container each fall, or plant it out into the garden in spring. Stand winter tubs in a reasonably sheltered sunny spot, ideally in front of a wall for extra protection, and raise the base of the container up on 'pot feet' or bricks so that excess water can drain away.

Container plants

Choose only the best plants for containers as they are always 'on show'. Reject any without plenty of buds or any with unhealthy leaves. Anticipate problems if the soil is bone dry or plants appear neglected. Well cared for plants in bud with a few flowers just open and fresh green foliage are best buys. Before planting remove any dead flowers or yellow leaves.

1 *Gather together a large container, potting mix and a variety of plants. For a colorful formal display, choose a compact evergreen shrub, trailing ivies and winter-flowering annuals.*

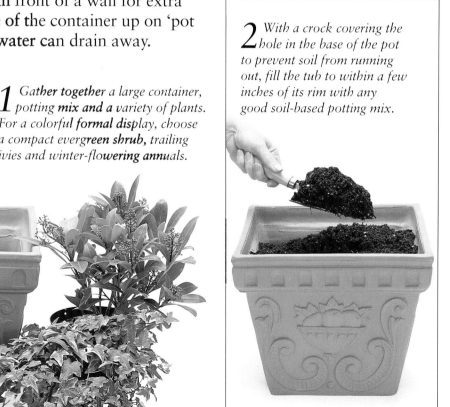

2 *With a crock covering the hole in the base of the pot to prevent soil from running out, fill the tub to within a few inches of its rim with any good soil-based potting mix.*

3 *First, put the largest plant in the center of the tub. Keep the rootball intact, as space will be short and there are several other plants to put in.*

Young, pot-grown winter-flowering evergreens, such as Skimmia japonica 'Rubella', look good in containers

Variegated ivy

Cultivated primrose hybrids (Primula acaulis hybrids)

4 A large plant, such as ivy, trailing over the tub, softens the straight edges and helps the evergreen to blend in with the arrangement.

5 Tuck flowering plants around the edge of the pot. Their colors should blend with the buds on the shrub.

6 Fit in as many flowering plants as possible. Once in bloom, they do not grow any more, so the finished result must provide the full impact.

7 Pull out strands of ivy for a wispy effect. Sit the arrangement in a prominent position. Water in well. Apply a weak feed during mild spells.

55

A pot of winter heathers

Larger, low-level containers, such as windowboxes, tubs and troughs, allow for more expansive winter displays based around heathers. You can combine heathers with miniature conifers, small plants of evergreen shrubs, such as *Fatsia japonica* or variegated *Euonymus,* and evergreen grasses or alpines, and even tuck in temporary pots of flowering spring bulbs. If you use ericaceous potting mix, which winter heathers and conifers will not mind sharing, you can include lime-hating plants, such as *Skimmia* or *Gaultheria procumbens* for flowers or berries; both associate well with heathers. In mild city centers, nearly hardy indoor plants, such as winter cherry *(Solanum capsicastrum)* and Indian azalea *(Rhododendron simsii),* could add a festive touch. Heathers can be difficult to team successfully with other plants, so stand plants together to test the effect of the group before buying. A fairly formal arrangement suits these types of plants best. In a large container, aim for a group of three upright evergreens of different heights with a carpet of heathers around it and other plants grouped amongst them. In a windowbox or trough, a row of identical evergreens or plants gently graduating to a central peak looks attractive.

4 *The conifer will form the center-piece. Position it so that the top of the rootball is about 0.5in(1.25cm) below the rim of the container.*

1 *Team flowering heathers with a container in a matching color; go for frostproof ceramics. Even the conifer has reddish-purple stems and tinted foliage.*

2 *Cover the drainage hole with a 'crock' to contain the potting mix. Alternatively, use small gauge wire gauze, which also keeps out worms.*

3 *Fill one third of the container with potting mix. Ericaceous mix is not necessary, as winter heathers do not mind a little lime in their soil.*

6 If the container is to stand against a wall, group the heathers more to the front and move the conifer closer to the back of the pot to make more room.

5 *Firm the conifer down gently. Space the heathers evenly around it, squeezing the rootballs slightly to make them fit into the pot.*

7 *Fill the spaces between the heathers with extra potting mix until the container is loosely filled to just below the rim. This prevents the roots from drying out.*

Chamaecyparis thyoides 'Purple Heather'

Erica darleyensis 'Darley Dale'

Erica carnea 'Rosalie'

Erica carnea 'March Seedling'

Winter care

Site the container where it can be easily seen from the house. Although heathers and conifers are quite tough, stand the pot in a reasonably sheltered spot if it includes spring bulbs and alpines Do not assume that winter rains will take care of watering for you. Check the potting mix every week and water whenever it starts to feel dry just below the surface. In a windy spot, the potting mix will dry out faster so water more often. Feed in mild spells in spring with a general-purpose liquid feed or add slow-release fertilizer granules to containers when planting.

8 *Water thoroughly and sit the pot on a matching saucer in its final position to create a colorful display.*

1 *Assemble the ingredients; be sure to remove plants from their pots before planting them. Despite its name, 'Golden King', the standard holly is a female that bears red berries if there is a male holly nearby.*

A festive winter arrangement

Evergreens form the basis of many pretty winter container arrangements, so why not consider making one specially with Christmas in mind? Festive foliage of holly and ivies forms the basis of this winter container display, backed up by traditional berries and evergreen foliage, plus an ornamental cabbage, which makes a long-lasting alternative to winter flowers. (Ornamental cabbages last until early spring, when they run to seed. They are not inhibited by bad weather, so you get a more reliable display.) If you cannot find a standard holly, you could use a poorly shaped bush and simply remove all but one of the stems to convert it into an instant standard. Alternatively, use a standard trained bay tree or a bushy holly with fewer surrounding plants. For a formal entrance, make a pair of matching pots and place one on either side of a porch. For a less formal look, team a single container with smaller but matching pots of evergreens, winter-flowering heathers and early spring bulbs. To keep winter displays looking their best, keep them in a well-sheltered spot, with containers raised up on pot feet out of puddles, and in as much light as possible. Even plants that normally prefer partial shade will thrive in better light during the dull winter days. Check containers regularly, even in winter, to see if they need watering; normal rainfall may not be able to get through the dense covering of foliage and into the potting mix. Feed during mild spells in spring. Pick off discolored leaves and generally tidy up container displays every week to keep them looking their best.

2 *Cover the drainage hole with a crock or flat stone and part fill the pot with potting mixture, but leave enough room for the plant roots.*

3 *Stand the holly in the very center; add the golden tree heather at the base to soften the strong upright line of the trunk. Firm in gently.*

4 Now add the Gaultheria and flowering heather to the front of the display, tucking potting mixture around their roots and firming them into place. Allow them to overflow the front of the pot.

5 Plant the taller ornamental cabbage in at the back of the display and add the trailing ivy, allowing the trails to curl round the sides of the pot towards the front. This gives an impression of instant maturity.

6 Stand the display on pot feet, say by a front door. Water well in and check weekly to make sure it does not dry out. No feeding will be needed until spring.

Ilex *x* altaclerensis 'Golden King'

Erica arborea 'Albert's Gold'

Gaultheria procumbens (checkerberry or partridge berry)

Ornamental cabbage

Hedera helix 'Sagittifolia' has long, narrow, arrowhead-shaped leaves,

Calluna vulgaris 'Alexandra'

A shallow bowl for winter

A shallow container makes a pleasant change from the usual pot-shaped types normally used for year-round plant displays, and teams well with more traditional types of arrangements to form an attractive group. The display shown here would, for instance, look very good teamed with the tall festive display featuring a standard holly tree as shown on page 58. Since shallow bowls dry out quickly, check them more often than usual to see if they need watering. And since they contain less potting mixture than a deeper container, they quickly become potbound (packed solid with roots) and the plants can become 'starved' of plant foods. Because of this, it makes sense to keep a potted display only for a single season before removing the plants and putting them out into the garden. When choosing plants to make up a winter arrangement, select those that are just coming up to their best, with flower buds beginning to open or foliage at its peak. Avoid small plants or those with obvious disease or damage. Completely fill the container, as the plants will not grow much more until the next growing season. Stand year-round containers of evergreens, heathers or conifers in a sunny but well-sheltered spot for the winter, raised up on pot feet to improve drainage. A site close to the house is best, since this is naturally sheltered by nearby walls, and in any case makes it easier to enjoy the containers without having to go outdoors.

Seasonal displays

Reasonably priced, ready-planted seasonal displays of small shrubs in containers are often available in garden centers. Enjoy them for the season and then plant them out in the garden. (This can be a cheap way of acquiring new plants.) Replant the container.

3 Knock the plants out of their pots and sit the largest - here the Aucuba - in the center. Add smaller plants with contrasting shapes and leaf textures around the edge.

1 Choose a good-quality frost resistant bowl and cover the drainage hole with a crock or flat stone to stop the potting mix trickling out, whilst still allowing excess water to drain away.

2 Scoop enough potting mix into the container to roughly half-fill it, leaving plenty of room for the plant rootballs. Any good potting mixture will do, either soil- or peat-based.

4 Add a trailing plant (here we have used a Carex) to dangle over one side of the pot and center the Skimmia just in front of the Aucuba, as this will become the strongest attraction.

Chamaecyparis lawsoniana 'Ellwood's Pillar'

Aucuba japonica 'Windsor Form'

Thuja orientalis 'Aurea Nana'

Skimmia reevesiana

Euonymus fortunei 'Blondie'

Carex oshimensis 'Evergold'

Erica vagans 'George Underwood'

Winter-flowering pansies

Calluna vulgaris 'Alexandra'

5 Fill in any gaps around the edge of the pot, especially at the front, with flowering heathers. They will balance the effect of the red skimmia berries.

6 Reserve a space at the front for a handful of winter pansies. They will continue flowering through the winter. Deadhead them regularly.

7 Water the arrangement and stand it on a doorstep, by a porch or on the patio. Team it with other seasonal containers for greater effect.

61

Space-saving vegetables

Small-scale gardeners regularly complain that they have no room to grow vegetables, but why not grow a few of your favorite edible crops in containers? Large tubs, troughs, and growing bags are all useful ways of converting 'wasted' space into productive cropping area. All you need is a narrow strip along a path, in a corner of a patio or even on a balcony, windowbox or flat roof (if it is sufficiently strong and has easy access). Do not bother with crops that take up a great deal of space or are cheap to buy in the shops; go for those that taste best picked garden-fresh. French beans, outdoor cucumbers, tomatoes, baby new potatoes, peppers, frilly red lettuce and golden courgettes, herbs and salad leaves, such as rocket and purslane, are all ideal choices. Growing bags and containers of potting mixture can be used several times over, as long as you plant completely different crops each time. Plant cucumbers, tomatoes or peppers first, as these are most sensitive to root problems, and follow with spinach, courgettes, potatoes and lettuce. Keep crops regularly fed from planting onwards, especially when reusing old potting mixture. Feed heavy-fruiting crops, such as tomatoes and peppers, with liquid tomato feed, and leafy crops including lettuce, beans and cucumbers, with general-purpose liquid feed. Stand containers of vegetables in a sheltered sunny spot, and check them daily to see if they need watering. Growing bags are particularly prone to drying out quickly when crops are tall and putting on rapid growth.

1 You can hide highly colored growing bags in a suitably sized, free-standing trough. Start cutting into the plastic with a pair of scissors.

2 In a trough, the sides of the bag are supported, so you can cut out the top of the bag completely, which gives you a much larger planting area.

3 Turn back the edges of the plastic to form a raised 'lip', which helps prevent water running off - a common problem when watering growing bags.

4 Knock the plants out of their pots and plant without disturbing the rootballs. These are bush courgette plants; plant two per growing bag.

Beans in a growing bag

Dwarf and climbing beans do well in growing bags. Water in and start feeding with general-purpose liquid feed weekly after three weeks. Dwarf beans need no support, but place climbers alongside a wall with trellis or wire netting for them to grow up, or make a framework of canes to stand over the bag.

Plant two rows of six plants down each side of the bag.

Above: *'Sugar snap' peas have an excellent taste and do well in growing bags. They need a sheltered, sunny site. Put plants out in late spring or sow seeds into the bags then.*

Peppers in a growing bag

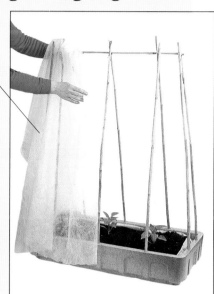

The fleece allows light to penetrate, but protects plants.

Right: *Plant three pepper plants per growing bag. The plants need plenty of warmth and shelter, so make a frame-work of canes and fix crop protection fleece over like a 'tent' until the weather warms up.*

Below: *Plant three tomato plants per bag. Bush varieties are best outdoors, but support them on canes. These slip into holes in the walls of this trough, which is made to take growing bags.*

5 *After planting and gently firming in, water the soil well so that it is evenly moist. Then water sparingly until plants are growing faster, when they will need more frequent watering.*

Growing potatoes in a tub

Sit each potato with the end containing the 'eyes' uppermost.

You can grow all kinds of potatoes in containers, but it is more practical to grow early (new) potatoes or 'specialist' varieties that are difficult to find in the shops. Early varieties can be produced even earlier than usual by planting the tubers six weeks earlier than recommended and keeping the container in a frost-free greenhouse or sunroom until after the last frost. Then move the container outdoors. Expect to gather the crop in early midsummer, leaving the container free to be planted up with flowers or other edibles, such as herbs. It is also possible to enjoy 'new' potatoes later in the season by storing a few seed potatoes of an early variety in a cool, shady spot and planting them after gathering the first crop of earlies. These will be ready to harvest from the fall onwards. However, remember to bring the container back into a frost-free growing environment before the first frosts, as potatoes are not hardy. Specialist gourmet potatoes grown for their fine flavor include both early and maincrop varieties. 'Belle de Fountenay', 'Pink Fir Apple' and 'Linzer Delikatess' are especially tasty. Early potatoes are ready to pick when the first flowers appear on the plants. There is no need to pull up the whole plant; just feel round for the largest potatoes and leave the others to grow for a bit longer. Leave maincrop potatoes until the foliage starts to yellow naturally before pulling them up, but again you can take a few potatoes before this stage. Keep potatoes well fed and watered during the growing period and buy new seed potatoes the following year.

1 *Buy seed potatoes in early spring and sit them on end to sprout. Keep them at cool to normal room temperature in daylight.*

2 *Shovel 3in(7.5cm) of potting mixture into the bottom of a large container. You could reuse old growing bag soil, as long as it has not been used for growing potatoes before.*

3 *When the sprouts on the seed potatoes are 0.5-1in(1.25-2.5cm) long, lay them on the soil in the tub, about 10in(25cm) apart, with the sprouts facing upwards. This tub is big enough to take three.*

Choose healthy tubers with no cuts and bruises, rotten bits or mold on the surface. Damaged tubers are more likely to rot than grow.

4 For maximum productivity, fit in a second 'tier' of potatoes. Shovel another 2in(5cm) of potting mixture into the tub, just deep enough to bury the first lot of potatoes.

5 Place another three potatoes, spaced as before, into the gaps between the potatoes in the previous layer. This way, the tub will be virtually full of potatoes.

6 Fill the tub with soil to within 1in(2.5cm) of the rim to allow for watering. Stand the tub in a sunny sheltered spot outside. Protect from frost.

Left: *Early potato varieties are ready when flowers appear. Do not pull up main crop potatoes until the leaves start yellowing in late midsummer.*

7 Thoroughly moisten the soil, but do not overwater - the tubers take a few weeks to root. When the shoots appear, feed and water regularly.

8 When the plants are growing strongly, keep them regularly watered and feed every 10 days with any good, general-purpose liquid feed.

Broad beans in a tub

Broad beans are so easy to cultivate that there really is no reason at all why you should not grow them, even if you have insufficient space in the garden, as they make splendid plants for growing in containers of all sorts on a sunny patio. The main thing to remember is that you must stick to the dwarf-growing varieties. These are short and sturdy and generally need no support, whereas the normal tall ones do. Choose 'The Sutton' for this type of gardening. The other important point is that you must never grow broad beans under cover once they are more than about 4in(10cm) tall. Any extra warmth will draw them up, so that very soon they become leggy and topple over. Make sure you keep them outdoors, so that the flowers are adequately pollinated by bees.

Because the dwarf varieties are not sufficiently hardy to withstand the winter outdoors, and will become drawn if grown in any heat, you should sow them in the early spring. Unfortunately, this means that they are as susceptible to attacks of blackfly in the summer as are all the other spring varieties (Longpod and Windsor types). Luckily, this pest is easy to control. Besides removing the tip of each shoot once young beans are forming, spray any affected plants with a suitable chemical that will destroy aphids (greenfly and blackfly). Any systemic insecticide will do this, but a spray containing just pirimicarb is more acceptable as it only kills the aphids and nothing else.

1 *Fill the container almost full with a good multipurpose potting mixture. Firm it down gently at this stage to prevent later compaction.*

2 *This is a dwarf variety 'The Sutton'. Sow the seeds individually on the surface about 4in(10cm) apart. Taller varieties are not suitable for containers.*

3 *Push the seeds into the potting mixture with your finger so that they end up 1.5-2in (4-5cm) deep. Move some soil back over the seeds and firm in gently.*

Above: *Children enjoy planting the large seeds of broad beans. The seeds are easy to handle and you can expect them all to germinate.*

4 *Water thoroughly. Do the initial watering in easy stages but do not stop until some drains out of the base.*

5 *Now you can see the benefits of growing only dwarf varieties. The plants stay short and are much better suited to growing in containers.*

6 *The young plants growing away well and in flower. When grown outside (cooler than under cover), this variety should need no support.*

Tomatoes in a growing bag

One of the best ways of growing tomatoes, in a greenhouse and outdoors, is in a growing bag. Tomatoes are susceptible to root diseases and greenhouse plants are especially vulnerable. Growing bags are free of pests and diseases and the plastic isolates plant roots from any diseased soil. Both single stem (disbudded) and bush varieties grow well in bags; raise the plants in a greenhouse or indoors on a windowsill. Generally speaking, grow one less plant of a bush variety than a disbudded one, because a bush type takes up more room. Follow the general rules for watering growing bags; wait until the surface of the soil has dried out and then give at least a gallon(4 liters) of water at a time. Feeding is not necessary for the first few weeks, but once the first fruits are pea-sized, feed according to the instructions on the bag or the bottle. To allow sun and air to reach the bottom fruits, remove the leaves from the base of the plant up to the lowest truss that has fruit showing red. Tomatoes dislike high growing temperatures, so make sure that the greenhouse is adequately ventilated and shaded. Too much heat leads to excessive water loss and this can cause problems, notably blossom end rot.

3 *Firm the plant gently but adequately into place. Never push the soil down too hard or you run the risk of it becoming waterlogged.*

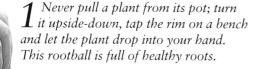

1 *Never pull a plant from its pot; turn it upside-down, tap the rim on a bench and let the plant drop into your hand. This rootball is full of healthy roots.*

2 *Scoop out a planting hole in the growing bag. This usually means going right down to the bottom to get it deep enough.*

When to plant out tomatoes

The tomato below is too young to plant out. Extra growth induced by putting it into new soil will lead to an unfruitful bottom truss. The tomato at right has the first flower open and is ready to plant out.

4 Put in three plants per bag in a greenhouse. Outdoors, plant four single stem, but only three bush plants per bag.

5 Apply up to 1.5 gallons(6 liters) of water at the first watering. Later waterings can be slightly less.

6 The same growing bag some weeks later. Being a bush variety, the side shoots have not been removed from the plant, so flowers abound with the promise of a good crop.

Above: *The tomatoes on this bush variety are maturing, providing an attractive array of colors from pale green to bright red. Single stem varieties in growing bags in a greenhouse should grow to six or seven fruit trusses high; outdoors expect to ripen four or five trusses. In both cases, nip out the plant at two leaves above the top truss.*

69

Planting strawberries in a growing bag

Growing bags allow you to garden on balconies and paving where there is no soil. They are cheaper than containers filled with potting mixture, as the packaging forms its own 'free' disposable container. Laid end to end, they can create what is effectively a continuous bed along a wall or on a patio and are the perfect way to grow shortlived fruit crops, such as strawberries. To grow strawberries, plant ten young, pot-grown plantlets per bag in spring. The nutrients in the potting mix provide all they need until flowering time, when you should start weekly liquid feeding with a half-strength, high-potash (tomato) feed. Continue feeding after picking the fruit until the end of the growing season. The following year, start feeding as soon as the plants make new growth in spring, as before. This time, after fruiting, discard both the old plants and bag, which you can tip on the garden to improve the soil, and start afresh the following spring. If there is space in a greenhouse or conservatory in early spring, you can 'force' growing bags of strawberries to give early fruit. Wait until a few weeks after midwinter, by which time the plants will have experienced a cold spell, then move them under cover. Hand-pollinate the flowers with a soft brush, as few bees will get in. The higher the temperature, the earlier the plants will crop, but even in an unheated greenhouse, fruit will ripen several weeks earlier than outside.

Above: Alpine strawberries have much smaller fruit then normal kinds, but a distinctive wild strawberry taste. They grow well in slight shade.

1 To conceal the rather 'loud' plastic packaging of the growing bag, it has been placed inside a special growing bag container. Made of tinted plastic, the effect is surprisingly natural.

2 As this growing bag is standing in a container, you can cut open the entire top instead of cutting as directed by the manufacturer. This gives a large open area for planting.

3 Knock ten plants out of their pots without breaking up the rootballs, and make a planting hole with a trowel.

4 Plant two rows of five, keeping each row close to the very edge of the growing bag to avoid over-crowding. Both rows can be of the same variety or plant one row of an early and one row of a maincrop.

5 After planting, water lightly in. Avoid overwatering as there are no drainage holes. When flowers appear, start feeding weekly with tomato feed.

Planting up a parsley pot

3 Once you have released each plant by upturning and tapping the pot, you may need to squeeze the rootball slightly to make it fit through the holes in the parsley pot. Avoid damaging the roots.

Parsley is probably one of the most used herbs in the kitchen; a vital ingredient in stuffings, marinades and bouquet garnis, and invaluable as a garnish. However, it does not dry well, becoming virtually tasteless, so it is well worth growing it yourself to ensure a fresh supply. Parsley can be chopped and frozen for adding to soups, stews and marinades, but you can still eat it fresh throughout the winter by sowing seeds in the greenhouse in midsummer or potting up the roots of spring-grown plants to bring indoors. Cropping plants by the handful rather than the sprig can quickly outstrip supply if your garden is small. If space is limited, the answer might be multi-pocketed strawberry barrels, which suit parsley just as well and are perfect for backyards and patios. You can buy them in terracotta or plastic; alternatively, make your own from an old wooden barrel. A partly shady spot is ideal for parsley and be sure to provide plenty of moisture. Parsley is a biennial and the leaves taste best in the first year, becoming bitter and rather coarse in the second, so try to sow a fresh supply each year in spring and late summer. The seeds can take at least six weeks to germinate, but this can be speeded up by soaking them overnight in warm water and then soaking a fine tilth seed bed with boiling water before planting. Cover the seeds thinly with fine soil and thin the seedlings to about 10in(25cm) apart.

Support the plant gently in your hand as you make it ready for planting.

The dense foliage of curled parsley (Petroselinum crispum) looks best in this kind of container.

1 *Place a few crocks or broken pieces of china in the bottom of the pot to ensure that the drainage holes do not become blocked.*

2 *Fill the pot with potting mix until you nearly reach the level of the planting spaces - in taller pots, these might appear at various heights.*

4 *Insert the parsley plants into the planting holes, pressing them firmly into the potting mixture. Make sure that the rootball is covered and the plants are the right way up.*

5 *Place the final plant in the top of the container, making sure that it is planted at the correct height to grow right out of the top.*

6 *After filling and firming with potting mixture, sprinkle a handful of small stones or gravel on the surface to reduce moisture loss.*

Parsley seeds or seedlings are both suitable for planting.

7 *The finished pot provides plenty of parsley for picking within a very small planted area. Pinch off flower stalks as they appear to maintain good growth.*

Potted herbs

At one time the only flowering plants seen in the cottage garden would have been herbs, or, loosely described, plants for a purpose; for medicinal use, personal or domestic hygiene or to add flavor to food. There was a vast range of these plants; although most have drifted back into the wild, others are the venerable predecessors of today's flower borders and many - in particular the culinary herbs - are enjoying an enthusiastic revival. Their appeal is multifaceted: they have beautiful and aromatic foliage to enhance the garden, properties to repel pests and protect other plants that are grown beside them, an irresistible attraction for bees and butterflies and they are essentially part of the lighter, healthier trend in cookery, with its emphasis on fresh vegetables and salads.

Some herbs are rampantly invasive and need to be sited very carefully away from the rest of the garden and out of the prevailing wind. Try containing them in pots on a bed of shingle, where the umpteen thousand seedlings can be easily hoed away. A basic collection of the most useful herbs would include parsley, thyme, sage, mint, bay, basil, marjoram, chives and fennel. Once you are acquainted with them, chervil, rosemary, tarragon, lovage and sorrel soon become 'must haves'.

Some herbs grown in containers will need to be renewed every two or three years. The woody ones, such as sage and rosemary, become sparse and leggy, while rampant spearmint and fennel get choked. However, marjoram, hyssop, sorrel, savory, tarragon and thyme, with their small roots and neat habit, will last for many years, just getting better.

Right: Potted lemon balm forms the center of this compact herb garden, which has been imaginatively planted as a patchwork in paving, where the herbs can be clipped and pinched to keep them in shape.

Flue liners are available in buff and terracotta, round or square.

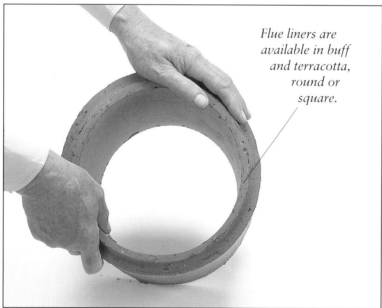

1 *In an open-ended pot, the roots can grow into the earth beneath. At 9in(23cm) or 12in(30cm) in diameter, flue liners are large enough to accommodate the most vigorous species.*

2 *Settle the base into the ground and fill it two-thirds full with good-quality garden soil. It is not a good idea to use potting mixture.*

Above: *Quite apart from its value as a culinary herb, golden marjoram makes a superb pot plant, flowering in mauve or white and very attractive to bees. Also makes excellent ground cover.*

Right: *Arrange the flue liners at varying heights, sinking some deeper into the ground than others. Put those herbs that enjoy moist conditions in the lower containers.*

3 Place the plant in the flue liner and water it. Top up the soil until it is 2in(5cm) below the rim of the liner to retain moisture when watered.

The flat-leaved parsley is a stronger plant with a better flavor than the curly-leaved variety.

If chives are left to dry out the plant will collapse. The flowers bloom in varying shades of lavender-pink in early summer and bees adore them.

The leaves of purple sage are as good in cooking as the common green one. It looks wonderful in the flower bed, with spikes of blue flowers in early summer.

Thymus doerfleri 'Bressingham Pink'

Creating a herb garden for the windowsill

A windowbox is the perfect way to grow a selection of culinary herbs in the minimum of space. The kitchen windowsill is an obvious site, providing the window opens conveniently enough for regular access to your mini garden. Make absolutely sure that the windowbox is firmly secured; use strong brackets or ties and check these periodically for wear or weathering. The box might be home-made from new or old timber, painted to match window frames or shutters; or it might be lightweight plastic, antique stone or terracotta. If the windows are too exposed a site, why not plant up an indoor windowbox, perfect for a few of the more tender species, such as basil. Regular cropping or trimming is important to ensure that the herbs remain small and leafy. Keep the box adequately watered and apply a liquid feed during the growing and cropping season. The soil soon runs out of essential nutrients in the confines of a box, especially where plants grow prolifically and where rain washes constantly through the soil. A mulch of small pebbles conserves moisture and reduces the effect of heavy rains.

1 Choose a selection of herbs - preferably with a variety of foliage shapes and textures - and stand them in the box or trough to see how they look together.

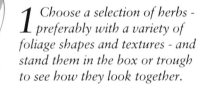

2 Take out the plants again and arrange a few crocks or broken pieces of pot in the bottom to prevent the potting mixture washing away.

3 Add 2-6in(5-15cm) of washed gravel or pea shingle to make a well-draining layer at the bottom of the box. Top up with planting mix.

4 Plant the herbs, keeping to your original plan and maintaining a balance of appearance, height and habit. Tip them gently out of their pots and into your hand, supporting the stem lightly between your fingers.

Herbs in the kitchen

The flavor of fresh herbs is far more delicate than that of dried ones, so use them generously. Generally speaking, add them at the end of cooking for maximum effect. Mint, basil and tarragon change their flavor once dried, so do not expect them to taste the same as before. Add fresh, chopped herbs with a swirl of cream to home-made soups; sprinkle them on salads; tie them in tiny bundles to add to stocks and stews; or tuck sprigs of rosemary, sage or thyme under the roast joint with a slice of unpeeled onion and a clove of garlic to bring out the flavor.

5 Top up with soil, making sure it settles between the plants without any air gaps. Do not fill right to the top of the box to allow for watering.

6 A sprinkling of gravel or small stones on top of the soil around the plants looks attractive and helps to slow down moisture loss.

Chives (Allium schoenoprasum)

Culinary thyme (Thymus vulgaris)

Sage (Salvia officinalis)

Parsley (Petroselinum crispum)

Sorrel (Rumex acetosa)

French tarragon (Artemisia dracunculus)

Oregano (Origanum vulgare)

7 The finished trough looks good and includes a useful blend of flavors for the cook. If you use plenty of herbs in cooking, reduce the number of plants in the box to two or three bigger plants.

A selection of herbs in containers

Lungwort
(Pulmonaria saccharata)

Golden feverfew,
(Tanacetum parthenium
aureum)

Variegated comfrey
(Symphytum grandiflorum)

Golden sage
(Salvia 'Icterina')

Broad leaf thyme
(T. pulegioides)

Purple-leaved violet
(Viola labradorica purpurea)

Rock hyssop
(Hyssopus aristatus)

Narrow leaf
golden marjoram
(Origanum
vulgare 'Aureum')

Compact marjoram
(O. compactum)

Thyme 'Rainbow Falls'

Red houseleek
(Sempervivum
tectorum rubra)

Thymus drucei minus

Golden lemon thyme
(Thymus x citriodorus 'Aureus')

Thyme
(T. vulgaris)

Parsley
(Petroselinum crispum)

French tarragon
(Artemisia dracunculus)

Mix and match

Choosing the right blend of herbs for your containers can be great fun. Even taking into account soil compatibility and whether the plants need sun or shade, there is plenty of scope to create pleasing contrasts of color, from darkest green to fresh lime; of foliage, from broadleaved to spiky or fleshy; and of size, from tall to tiny trailing varieties.

Sage
(Salvia officinalis)

Lavender
(Lavandula spica 'Munstead')

Tricolor sage
(Salvia officinalis 'Tricolor')

Calamint
(Calamintha grandiflora)

Tricolor sage
(Salvia officinalis 'Tricolor')

Artemisia
(Artemisia lanata pedamonta)

Bugle (Ajuga reptans 'Burgundy Glow')

Thymus doerfleri 'Bressingham Pink'

Thyme
(T. serpyllum rosea)

Thyme
(T. herba-barona)

79

Shaping a box tree

Box is a very popular and easily managed traditional topiary subject. Use *Buxus sempervirens* and not the miniature cultivar 'Suffruticosa'. To shape existing box bushes growing in the garden or fair-sized bushy plants from garden centers, the best technique is to choose a plant that already suggests a simple shape, such as a bun or sphere, and simply exaggerate that by regular light clipping. The easiest way to create more complicated shapes is to start with a very small plant or, better still, rooted cuttings. Cuttings can be taken from established box plants at any time during the late spring and summer period. Snip 3in(7.5cm) pieces from the tips of the shoots and remove the lower leaves. Push them to two-thirds their length into pots or trays of seed potting mixture. Keep them moist and shady. When rooted - usually six to eight weeks later - pot each cutting into a 4in(10cm) pot and pinch out the growing tip to make it grow bushy. Nip out the tips of the subsequent side shoots so that the young plant is bushy from the base. Then start training.

1 Start with a strong, rooted box cutting. Neatly nip off the growing tips of the shoots, using forefinger and thumbnail in a pincer movement. Repeat when the side shoots are 1in(2.5cm) long.

2 Use secateurs to nip back the tips of the next crop of sideshoots, so that each time the new growth reaches 2in(5cm) long it is shortened.

3 This regular pruning makes the plant bushier each time. At the same time as shortening the new growth, begin to roughly form the basic outline of the required shape.

4 Do not worry too much at this stage if the results are not very precise. The important thing is to have plenty of side shoots growing out in all directions.

5 As the first pot becomes filled with roots, move the plant into a larger pot with fresh potting mix to keep it growing well. Continue clipping regularly with small shears.

6 By now, it should be possible to see a distinct shape emerging from the plant. Frequent clipping is very important while the shape is being formed, so that side shoots are regularly 'stopped' to keep the growth bushy and dense.

7 When it reaches the required size, clip back to the previous outline each time. By then, clipping three or four times a year should be enough.

8 Once large enough to clip, trim the tips of the young shoots back just enough to encourage branching, which gives a dense leafy shape, while allowing the shape to grow in size.

Above: *Box balls in containers set out in a gap between clipped box hedges make a focal point in a formal setting.*

9 It is possible to create a good box ball about 9in(23cm) across using this method in three years. Clip two or three times a year to retain the shape and size thereafter.

81

Trimming a bay tree

Bay trees are traditionally trained into various ornamental shapes: standard 'lollipops' and pyramids are popular. These are often grown in terracotta pots by a doorway or on a patio, or used to decorate a formal herb garden. Unlike box, bay has large leaves so it is not clipped with shears but pruned with secateurs, or even 'finger pruned' by nipping out the very tips of the shoots while they are tiny, to encourage branching. The large leaves also make bay unsuitable for training into very detailed shapes, such as spirals or peacocks, as it is not possible to achieve such a neat outline as with a small-leaved subject. However, it makes sense to train a bay tree, especially in a small garden, otherwise it quickly grows into a large untidy bush. A potted tree can be moved under cover during spells of cold, windy weather in winter, which might otherwise cause the ends of the branches to die back, or the evergreen foliage to be browned and spoiled.

1 To trim a pyramidal tree, such as this bay, make a tripod of canes and slip it over the tree so you can see at once which shoots are growing outside the required shape. Use a hoop of stiff wire to encircle the tree, outside the canes, as an adjustable pruning guide to ensure you end up with an even, conical shape.

2 Since bay leaves are quite big and their appearance would be spoiled if leaves were cut in half, it is best to prune them with secateurs instead of clipping them with shears.

4 The end result is a smartly trimmed bay tree. Do not expect to achieve a totally smooth outline, as you could with a small-leaved plant that has been clipped.

Above: *Pinch out the tips of young shoots growing towards the edge of the desired shape.*

Move the wire hoop to the area you are working on so you can constantly check what the ideal outline shape should be as you are pruning.

As a bonus, you can dry the bay prunings and use them fresh or dried in cookery.

3 Using the cane tripod as a guide, snip away any shoots that extend beyond the pyramidal outline, cutting just beyond a leaf so there are no bits of bare twig sticking out.

Here the pot is standing inside a terracotta pot cover. Do not plant into a rounded pot, as you cannot get the rootball out without breaking the pot.

Creating a bonsai conifer

Good plants for an oriental-style garden include flowering cherry, almond, peach, ornamental quince *(Chaenomeles)*, rhododendron and azalea, bamboo and Japanese maple (*Acer palmatum* cultivars). Evergreens and conifers can be trimmed into approximations of bonsai shapes, even when they are growing in the ground. Another effective way of trimming them is to leave bare stems at the base of the plant and clip the foliage to resemble 'clouds' at the top. Good conifers for clipping include the blue-leaved *Chamaecyparis pisifera* 'Boulevard' and dwarf cultivars of *C. lawsoniana*, such as 'Green Globe'. Trees and shrubs that grow naturally into dramatic bonsai-like shapes without any need to prune or train them include the dwarf Mount Fuji cherry (*Prunus incisa* 'Kojo no Mai'), twiggy, upright *Prunus* 'Amanogawa', contorted hazel, and unusual weeping conifers, such as *Sequoiadendron giganteum* 'Pendulum'. Poorly shaped specimens of azalea and other oriental-look shrubs can be a cheap buy in garden centers and are easily pruned into lopsided 'bonsai' type shapes. A small collection of real bonsai trees in traditional tiny containers displayed on shelves or staging adds interest to this type of garden, but are best left to enthusiasts, as they need regular root pruning, wiring and daily watering. You can achieve a similar effect by growing traditional bonsai subjects (conifers, wisteria, oak, acers, pines, etc.) in much larger pots, in the same way as you would grow shrubs on a patio. These can be trimmed into freehand oriental shapes, just for fun.

1 Small and medium-sized conifers can easily be converted into potted oriental styles. It is a good way to use a less than perfect specimen.

2 Trim away the lower leaves to accentuate the trunk-like appearance of the lower stem, removing all dead leaves and shoots.

3 Prune out all brown leaves and bare shoots, so that everything left is green and healthy. Now you can start trimming.

4 Spread out the main branches to see the basic structure and decide how to shape it.

5 *Thin out some of the growth from the base of the plant to start exposing the outline of the main branches growing out from the 'trunk'. The ultimate aim is to create a plant with a craggy, aged look.*

6 *Move to the top of the plant and thin the top to accentuate the shape of the main branches, leaving 'key' fronds of foliage towards the end of each large shoot.*

7 *Continue to thin out the plant. The aim is to produce an asymmetrical shape that looks as if it has been naturally sculpted by the wind. Shorten some shoots to leave stubs along the branches, for character.*

Chamaecyparis pisifera 'Boulevard Variegated'

Rubbing the scales off the stems gives them a smoother finish.

8 *Stop when you think you have done enough. The finished tree should have a good basic framework of exposed branches with a well-balanced spread of foliage towards the tips.*

85

Hebe and ginkgo in oriental style

2 Bend the horizontal shoots over and tie them in place to accentuate the effect.

1 Ginkgo biloba, *the prehistoric maidenhair tree, is a good choice for clipping into an oriental-inspired shape. This one is not a good specimen for normal use, but just right for creating an oriental look.*

Some conifers and evergreens naturally grow into striking shapes that make them suitable for an 'oriental' display without much clipping and trimming. Alternatively, you could group a collection of choice, truly dwarf conifers and evergreens on a patio in matching weatherproof pots for a low-maintenance, all-year-round display. For compact, globular shapes, go for *Chamaecyparis* 'Gnome' and *Hebe* 'Green Globe'; for a compact craggy spire choose *Chamaecyparis obtusa* 'Tetragona Aurea', or for shaggy curls go for *Pinus mugo* 'Pumilio'. Since these are not being treated as true bonsai trees, choose pots of a suitable size for each plant and a soil-based potting mixture. After a year or two, the plants will need moving to a pot one size larger, preferably in spring. When a plant reaches the maximum desired size, repot it back into the same pot after trimming away about one quarter of the fine roots from the edge of the rootball.

Trimming a hebe

1 This Hebe 'Green Globe' *has a naturally tight, compact shape that needs little trimming. Just tidy up the new growth.*

2 Use single-handed *clippers, sheep shears or even large scissors to give it a 'haircut'. Snip back the new growth to re-establish the solid outline. Start at the top of the plant.*

3 Curve the top and *progress to the sides, keeping carefully to the natural shape of the plant. Trim the plant once a year just after the main flush of growth to keep it neat.*

3 Pull down the two shoots so that they lie roughly parallel, with one echoing the curve of the other. The shape should have 'set' within a year, and then you can remove the string.

4 Move the tree into a larger oriental-style pot. The top of the rootball should lie flush with the soil surface just below the rim of the new container.

5 Before completing potting, experiment by tipping the tree to see if you can create a better 'bonsai shape' by inclining the stem at an angle. An irregular shape often looks best.

4 New growth will soften the hard edges. Side shoots will appear from just below the cut ends, making a bushier shape.

Acer palmatum 'Atropurpureum'

Maidenhair tree (Ginkgo biloba)

Hebe 'Green Globe'

Part Two

HANGING BASKETS AND WINDOWBOXES

Hanging baskets, wall pots and windowboxes allow you to cultivate what is to all intents and purposes a hostile environment - the wall of a house is like a sheer cliff face with no toeholds! But fix in a few screws, hooks and brackets and you can transform bare bricks into luxuriant hanging gardens.

The wonderful thing about these containers is that the display is only temporary. You can ring the changes from year to year and from season to season and have great fun experimenting with different plants and color schemes. Once you branch out into using plants other than those traditionally associated with baskets and windowboxes, the palette of colors and textures available increases enormously. Baskets, wall pots and windowboxes are available in a wide range of materials and designs, some more practical than others. On the following pages you will find advice on lining and hanging up baskets, and creative and practical ideas for painting designs on simple windowboxes.

There is no need to keep buying new containers. You can recycle the same container through the seasons, using a variety of colors and plant associations to produce strikingly different results each time. This section takes you through the seasons, with ideas on what plants are available at the time. Even in the depths of winter, you can enjoy wonderful displays of fresh flowers, colorful berries and foliage around the door.

Left: A windowbox of pink and red geraniums. **Right:** *A wall basket of trailing geraniums and variegated felicia.*

The new trailing petunia variety Surfinia 'Blue Vein'.

Where and how to hang your basket

Practicality and safety, aesthetics and the needs of your plants are the points to bear in mind when hanging a basket. Do not hang it where people will knock their heads on it, or so close to the door that you must fight your way through trailing foliage to get in and out; remember, baskets can grow considerably bigger than when first planted! Where space is limited, consider wall pots and baskets as a space-saving alternative. You need not always hang them from traditional brackets, either. On a pergola or porch, all you need to do is to screw sturdy hooks into the woodwork. Custom-built wall baskets usually come with screw holes, but you can fix ordinary round plants pots to the wall or drainpipes using specially designed clips. Where you position baskets can make all the difference to how easy they are to maintain and how well the plants perform. Baskets need almost daily attention - feeding, watering, deadheading - so hang them for easy access or fit pulleys for raising and lowering. Keep plants with similar requirements for light and moisture together, so that you can hang them where they will have the optimum conditions for growth.

Above: Trailing plants need plenty of space. Single-subject baskets such as this cascading petunia can be very effective, but must be grown to perfection, as there are no other plants to distract the eye.

Right: These cleverly designed coach lamps have hooks on which you can suspend hanging baskets. At night, the flowers will be illuminated, making a real welcome for visitors.

Left: A symmetrically planted wall basket on a central pillar between two doorways emphasizes the architectural detail perfectly. The verbena, petunia and variegated felicia in this basket all prefer a sunny position - only the tuberous begonias and ivy are tolerant of shade. In this case, a spot in good light out of strong midday sun would be ideal.

Fixing a bracket to a wall

Once filled with potting mixture and plants, hanging baskets can be surprisingly heavy, so it is important to fix the brackets properly. When attaching a bracket, you need to plug the hole to prevent the screw from working its way out (see below). Always use the correct size bracket for the basket. These are usually sold for a particular basket diameter, for example 12in(30cm), 14in(35cm), etc.

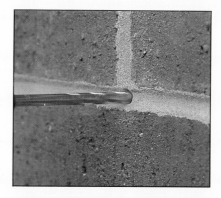

Left: Put the bracket against the wall and mark the position of the screw holes using a felt-tipped pen. Using a hammer-action drill and the correct sized masonry drill bit, drill the top hole.

Left: Push the wall plug into the hole and then put the bracket back in place. Fix the top screw loosely so that you can check the position of the second hole. Make any necessary adjustments.

Below: The traditional way to hang baskets is from a bracket fixed to a wall or fence. Brackets are available in many designs, some simple, some highly ornamental.

Right: Drill and plug the second hole and screw the bracket firmly in place. For fixing wall pots and baskets directly to a wall, follow the same steps for drilling and plugging.

91

Feeding and watering

Watering should be a daily or, better still, twice daily routine, especially for baskets in full sun or in a windy spot. Never rely on rainfall to do the job for you and do not wait for plants to wilt before attending to them. Some basket plants never fully recover and soilless compost is notoriously difficult to rewet once it has dried beyond a certain point. Luckily, there are several ways to make the job easier. You can buy easy-reach attachments for hose pipes and devices that allow you to raise or lower a basket for maintenance. The trick is to apply a slow, steady stream of water that has a real chance of soaking in. Do not assume that just because water starts running out, the basket has reached capacity. It is more effective to water several times through the day, using a small watering can, than to give baskets a quick deluge that inevitably results in the water pouring straight out. Use 14- or 16in(35 or 40cm) diameter baskets, rather than 12in(30cm) ones, unless you can guarantee adequate watering, and choose self-watering baskets if you are unable to water daily in summer. Once the feed in the potting mix has been used up (see back of bag for timings), begin to apply liquid feeds, usually once a week at full strength or every time you water, using roughly half the recommended dose. Too much leafy growth at the expense of flowers usually means that you are using a product with too high a proportion of nitrogen. Choose a fertilizer for bedding and other flowering plants. A slow-release fertilizer applied at the beginning of the season makes the job even easier.

Feeding your plants

Regular liquid feeding gives the best results, but if you do not have the time or are apt to forget, use slow-release feeding pellets or tablets. Insert these into the potting mix at planting time. They last the whole season, releasing feed when plants are watered. The amount varies according to the temperature.

A perforated plate covered with capillary matting separates the potting mixture from the reservoir.

Watering tube for filling reservoir.

A capillary matting wick draws the water up from the reservoir to the potting mixture.

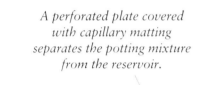

Self-watering hanging baskets have a hidden reservoir of water below the potting mix.

Left: *A plastic bottle cut in half, the pointed end buried in the soil at planting time, becomes a mini-reservoir that is soon hidden by the growing plants.*

Right: *Special long-lance attachments that fit onto a hose pipe allow you to reach up into high baskets. Using the on-off switch on the handle, you can deliver the water in small doses.*

Right: *An empty plastic bottle is also a useful aid to watering, especially if you just have one or two baskets. It is much lighter than a full watering can and is therefore ideal for overhead watering.*

Above: Easy-to-operate pulley systems clip onto the hanging hook or bracket and give access to baskets for feeding, watering and maintenance.

Above: *Reach up to the base of the basket and pull it down to attend to plants. Nudge the basket up to release the lock and push it back into place.*

Soaking a dried out hanging basket

1 Peat-based potting mix is very difficult to rewet if a basket has dried out. Water just tends to run straight through. If this happens, fill a sink or bowl with water and add a drop of liquid detergent to help the water 'stick' to the soil.

2 Plunge the basket into the water and leave it until the potting mix is completely saturated. Allow the basket to drain, then stand it in a sheltered, shady place until the plants recover. Cut off dead shoots and flowers before rehanging.

Maintaining your basket while you are away

The best solution to the problem of how to look after hanging baskets is a willing neighbor, but if you cannot arrange for someone to stand in for you until your return, then you will need to make other provisions. First, soak the baskets so that the soil is saturated with water and then put them down in a shady spot at floor level. Up on the wall they are much more exposed to drying elements - wind, sun and heat radiated back onto the basket from the wall. This procedure should keep baskets in reasonable condition for three or four days unless the weather is exceptionally hot. Even if someone is coming in to water, it is a good idea to do this, clustering the baskets together in one place for easy access. For longer periods, a little more preparation is required. 'Planting' baskets in a shady border is a good solution for maintaining traditional baskets lined with moss or another porous material, as moisture loss is dramatically reduced when the sides of the basket are surrounded by damp soil. Another technique is to set up some kind of automatic watering system, such as the capillary wick method, which is ideal for wall pots and baskets with solid sides. You can of course combine the two methods for traditional baskets. Whichever method you choose, be sure to remove flowers that will be over by your return and deal with any pest problems before you leave.

A capillary wick

A couple of days before leaving, cut a piece of capillary matting into a long strip. Soak it, push one end into the basket and leave the other end in water. Check that the plants take up the water.

1 Find a spot in a sheltered, shady part of the garden and dig a hole large enough to accommodate the base of the basket up to planting level.

2 Water the hole thoroughly and soak the basket in readiness for planting. You must ensure maximum saturation before you go away.

3 Sprinkle a few slug pellets into and around the hole and in the top of the basket to protect against attack. Check for slugs on your return.

5 *Drastic though it may seem, you must remove all the flowers. Bunch together the stems of small-flowered plants and cut them back near the base.*

6 *Take off any blooms that have just started to open and would be over on your return. Water the basket and surrounding soil once more.*

4 *Lifting trailers clear of the base, lower the basket into the prepared hole. Rest the hanging chain on the surface and then backfill with soil.*

Baskets sunk into damp soil and surrounded by plants in a shady border lose water much less rapidly than if left on a wall.

A self-watering spring basket

The capillary matting is in direct contact with the soil. If it is damp, so is the soil.

1 Feed the wick through the plastic base plate. It draws water up from the reservoir at the base of the basket and keeps the capillary matting damp.

For people who are out of the house all day or who are a little forgetful when it comes to watering, a self-watering hanging basket is the perfect solution. Immediately after planting, water the basket in the normal way to ensure that the potting mixture is thoroughly wetted. Thereafter, water will be drawn up from the reservoir at the bottom of the basket, as and when the plants require it. If you use the tube to fill the reservoir, there is no danger of over-watering, as seep holes in the sides allow the excess to drain out.

In this display, a fresh scheme of yellow and white spring flowers and foliage contrasts with the dark green basket. As it has solid sides, all the planting has to go in the top of the basket, so pick at least one plant with long trails to soften the edge. This green-and-white variegated ivy with its finely pointed leaves stands out beautifully. White drumstick primulas pick up on the white-edged ivy and make a striking and unusual centerpiece. Their display is relatively long-lived, the spherical heads opening and developing over a number of weeks. When flowering has finished, transfer the plants to the garden, if possible to a spot with moisture-retentive soil and light shade. The glossy-leaved *Euonymus japonicus* 'Aureus' comes from the houseplant section of a garden center as pots of rooted cuttings. When this basket is dismantled, it should be possible to separate these out and pot them up individually.

2 Push the watering tube through the hole in the base plate before adding potting mix and plants. You should be able to camouflage it easily.

3 Add a layer of moist potting mix, completely covering the capillary matting. Try the largest plant for size and adjust the level as necessary.

4 If the rootball is too big to fit in the basket, knock off any loose soil first and gently tease the roots apart at the base, so that they spread out flat.

Use a peat-based potting mixture formulated for hanging baskets.

Primula denticulata 'Alba' (white-flowered drumstick primula)

Primula (hardy hybrid primrose)

8 Hang the basket in a lightly shaded, sheltered spot. Continue watering via the tube. Remove individual blooms as they fade and cut off drumsticks when the whole head has finished flowering.

5 Add another primula and then fill in the gaps left on one side with the variegated euonymus. Put in more potting mix as you go.

Euonymus japonicus 'Aureus'

Hedera helix cultivar (variegated ivy)

7 Split apart a couple of pots of rooted ivy cuttings and fit them around the edge of the basket. Fill any gaps with soil. Water the potting mix thoroughly in the usual way.

6 Plant two hardy primroses, one on either side of the watering tube. Leave space around the rim for some trailing plants. As well as ivy, try variegated periwinkle, aubretia or silver lamium.

Hyacinths and primulas

This scheme is a rich blend of jewel-colored primulas, red hyacinths and warm terracotta, shades more often associated with late summer. The new *Primula* 'Wanda' hybrids have introduced a whole set of colors for the spring garden - glowing purples, reds and blues, often further enhanced by dark foliage. Mixed trays of plants may contain white-, yellow- and pink-flowered forms, so if you want to copy this scheme, wait until one or two buds have opened to check the color or buy plants separately in flower. Heavily scented hyacinths can often be bought in bud as single bulbs and add a luxurious touch to plantings of this kind. Like the hybrid primroses, hyacinths now come in many different colors, including orange and creamy yellow, though as potted bulbs, pinks, blues and white still predominate.

The advantage of buying plants in single colors is that color scheming in mixed arrangements is so much easier. There are several, equally effective ways to approach color scheming; one is to stick to just one color of flower, but to vary the form and texture of the plants as much as possible, say an all-white or all-yellow scheme. Another is to pick two strongly contrasting colors, such as orange and blue, purple and yellow or cerise-pink and lime-green. The color scheme chosen for this wall pot illustrates another option, namely a blend of related colors and shades. The reverse 'cool' option to the one illustrated would be blues, purples, silver-white and lime-green.

4 *Place the hyacinths against the back wall of the basket, leaving space for the primulas in the foreground. You may need to shake some of the potting mixture from around the roots to create more room.*

Be sure to moisten the potting mix before use.

1 *Line a terracotta wall basket with black plastic to prevent evaporation through the sides. Cut a hole in the base in line with the drainage hole.*

2 *Put a flat stone over the hole to prevent soil loss and then add a shallow layer of gravel to provide good drainage for the plants.*

3 *Cover the gravel with potting mix. Always use fresh potting mix and never garden compost or soil, which contains too many pests and diseases.*

5 Do not worry if the hyacinths look a little awkward at first; the primroses will soon cover up the base of the bulbs. Lay the plants out first, so that you can work out which are the best color combinations.

6 Squeeze the rootballs into an oval shape so that you can fit in as many plants as possible. Winter and spring baskets tend not to grow like summer ones, so cram them full for maximum impact.

Some more schemes for spring

Silver Cineraria, *pale blue pansies and white polyanthus.*

Velvet-red pansies with Heuchera '*Palace Purple*' *as the centerpiece; dark green ivy trails.*

White heather with Lamium '*White Nancy*'.

Festuca glauca *as the centerpiece with red* Bellis *(double daisies).*

Slate-blue polyanthus, cream Viola *and* Euonymus japonicus '*Aureus*'.

Pansy '*Imperial Antique Shades*' F1 *with blue-gray dwarf conifer.*

Reddish pink hyacinths

Primula '*Wanda*' *hybrid*

Terracotta wall basket with classical-style relief.

7 The primroses will flower for several weeks if they are regularly watered and dead-headed. Hyacinths, however, are not as long-lived. Once their flowers have faded, cut off the heads, but keep the leaves intact.

Buckets full of bulbs

Shiny metal pails make fun containers, especially for children's gardens, and are easily converted to hanging baskets with a length of silver-colored chain. This mixed planting of bulbs is unusual but works well because of the contrast of form and color. You can now buy a wide variety of potted bulbs, in bud or flower, between late winter and early spring. Dwarf varieties are particularly suited to hanging baskets, especially dwarf, multiheaded daffodils, grape hyacinths, chionodoxas, scillas and *Anemone blanda*, all of which flower over a relatively long period. Once flowering has finished, take the buckets off display, remove the faded heads and continue to feed and water, maintaining the foliage to allow the bulbs to build up reserves for flowering the following spring. As an alternative to bulbs, you could plant a whole collection of silver buckets with individual polyanthus or hardy primrose hybrids. Pick bright paintbox colors - red, yellow, blue and cerise for a cheerful welcome for visitors at the front of the house.

1 Put a layer of gravel or small pieces of broken styrofoam trays in the bucket to provide a drainage layer in these sealed containers.

Dividing clumps of bulbs

Provided you do not damage too many of the roots, you can separate out individual bulbs from their clumps quite safely. Water thoroughly a few hours beforehand to help them cope better with the stress.

__Right:__ Tease off as much soil as you can from the daffodil rootball, reducing its size to fit the bucket.

__Below:__ Gently pull apart the rootball, separating individual bulbs for planting in narrow gaps.

2 Add a little soil - use a gritty, free-draining mix if you do not intend to perforate the bucket base. Remove handles for easy planting.

Narcissus
'Tête à Tête'

6 *Hang the buckets at head height to appreciate the flowers at close quarters. If using multi-headed daffodils, such as 'Tête à Tête', pick off individual flowers as they fade.*

Chionodoxa luciliae

Muscari
armeniacum
(Grape hyacinth)

3 *Remove some soil from around the roots of the clump of daffodils. Plant the bulbs, leaving enough space around the edges for the muscari.*

4 *Using small, teased-out clumps or individual grape hyacinth bulbs, fill in round the edge of the daffodil centerpiece. Squeeze in as many bulbs as you can. The flower heads may droop a bit at first but should re-orientate themselves after a few days.*

5 *This time, using muscari for the central planting, make an outer ring of the smaller, pale blue-and-white striped chionodoxas. Cover any exposed roots or bulbs with more potting mix and water carefully to settle the soil. Take care not to overwater.*

1 *Line the back and base of the basket with black plastic, tucking the top edge in behind the frame at the back to stop it slipping down later on.*

A spring wall basket

A large, manger-style basket can create an impressive wall feature to brighten up a bare expanse of brickwork. It could also be used like a windowbox, fixed beneath the frame. Though not very wide, there is room along the length for a good assortment of plants and because there are gaps between the bars, you can plant through the front easily. Putting pink and yellow plants next to each other in the garden is normally frowned upon, but this scheme just goes to show how rules about color combinations can often be broken with great success! Using the same types of plant, there are several other colorways that work well. For example, if you want a more vivid scheme, try scarlet red tulips, such as the dwarf 'Red Riding Hood', white daisies, deep blue polyanthus and blue-and-white violas. More ideas are suggested in the panel.

The polyanthus used in this scheme are the exact color of wild primroses and to take the wild theme a step further, the spaces between all the plants were filled with moss, giving the impression of a bank in the hedgerow filled with spring flowers. With the exception of the tulips, the flowers in this basket will keep blooming for weeks, provided they have been looked after properly. If the leaves begin to yellow and show signs of starvation, water with a liquid feed. Deadhead regularly and keep a watch for aphids and other pests, which can proliferate without warning during warm spells.

2 *Lift up the lining and tuck some moss underneath to hide the plastic. Add a thick layer of moss until it is high enough to add the first plants.*

3 *Break up bedding strips of violas and feed them through the bars at different heights for a more natural effect. Fill the gaps in between with potting mix.*

Schemes for spring

Yellow dwarf daffodils, blue Scilla siberica or Muscari (grape hyacinth) and red primroses planted with gold variegated ivy or variegated Vinca minor.

Dark purple tulips, light purple and mauve-pink shades of dwarf wallflowers and silver cineraria planted with green-leaved Lamium maculatum.

Scarlet-red, double-flowered Ranunculus, maroon-red Heuchera 'Palace Purple' and deep red Dicentra 'Bacchanal' planted with dark green ivy.

White heathers, white polyanthus, white pansy, white Lamium 'White Nancy'.

Skimmia japonica 'Rubella', Euonymus 'Emerald Gaiety' and Vinca minor trails.

4 *Put three pots of tulips along the back, carefully breaking the roots apart so that the bulbs can be planted in more of a straight line, allowing room for the other flowers in the foreground.*

5 *Add the yellow polyanthus in a zigzag line, leaving gaps in between for the double daisies. You may need to squeeze the rootballs out of shape to fit them in.*

Tulipa kaufmanniana 'The First'

Polyanthus 'Crescendo Primrose'

6 *Fill in any spaces with double daisies. Add potting mix around the plants and firm in gently. Cover any gaps with sphagnum moss and water the arrangement thoroughly.*

Bellis perennis (*double daisy*)

7 *Once the tulips have started to fade, carefully lift them out intact and plant them in the garden, where they can continue to grow and build up reserves for the following year. Replace them with more pot-grown bulbs and some spring-flowering herbaceous plants.*

Viola

103

Silver baskets of campanulas

Planted up, a pair of these tiny woven silver baskets would make a lovely gift. For a more natural look, there are plenty of tiny wicker baskets available, but whatever you choose, both the planting and method of hanging need to be on the same Lilliputian scale. One basket on its own is unlikely to make sufficient impact, so try two or more baskets hung at different heights, say from a curtain pole across a small window. In spring, you will often find outdoor plants mixed in with the houseplants in garden centers. These are forced into flower early to be used for temporary indoor decoration and may be planted outside once the display has finished. Campanulas and a variety of bulbs make popular subjects for forcing. Here, the lilac-blue blooms of an alpine bellflower (*Campanula* sp.) combine beautifully with the silver of the basket. The flowers and leaves are naturally small-scale, but growers can now produce temporarily miniaturized plants that flower at only a few inches tall. If you like the idea of using dwarf bulbs in baskets, try potting some up in the fall and grow them on through the winter in a cold frame. Once you can see color in the flower buds, plant them in the baskets and bring them indoors. Try chionodoxa, scilla, crocus and puschkinia.

2 *To prevent drips, line the basket with a square of transparent plastic. Fold the corners to fit and trim off any excess at the top with scissors.*

3 *Add some gravel or charcoal chippings to provide drainage, but take care not to overwater, especially when using drought-tolerant plants.*

Campanula *sp.*
(alpine bellflower)

1 *Have the baskets to hand when choosing your plants and other materials, such as the ribbon, to see if the combinations will work well.*

4 Try the campanulas in the baskets to work out the best arrangement. There may not be room for any potting mix in the base.

6 Hang the baskets in a cool, well-lit position. Suspend them using fine florist's ribbon. If the baskets are a gift, you could add some extra ribbon loops and cork-screw curls to the handle as well.

5 Now plant the campanulas; allow some foliage to trail over the basket sides. Fill the gaps between plants with potting mix so that there are no air spaces. Add sufficient water to settle the soil.

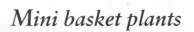

Mini basket plants

Cyclamen persicum (mini cyclamen)
Dendranthema (mini pot mum)
Exacum affine (mini Persian violet)
Kalanchoe blossfeldiana (mini flaming Katy), Rosa (mini rose)
Saintpaulia ionantha (mini African violet)
Houseplant 'tots' from garden centers make good, temporarily small, foliage plants for very small containers.

A cottage garden basket

This wicker basket has a rustic look, so the planting style is soft and relaxed, just like a traditional cottage garden border. *Campanula carpatica* 'Blue Clips', a hardy alpine bellflower that is sometimes brought into flower early and sold as a temporary indoor plant, is teamed with a gold-leaved trailing ivy. Plenty of other hardy herbaceous plants and tender perennials would produce a similar effect, including the dwarf marguerites (*Argyranthemum frutescens* cultivars, such as 'Petite Pink'), and dwarf scabious, *Scabiosa* 'Butterfly Blue' and 'Pink Mist', which flower over a long period. A semi-trailing fuchsia, such as the frilly-petalled 'Swingtime', would work well in combination with the trailing *Verbena* 'Sissinghurst' or paler pink 'Silver Anne', both vigorous and with a strong mildew resistance. Many hardy annuals, grown in pots and transferred to the basket when large enough, would also give the required 'cottage' look. Try *Nasturtium* 'Alaska', with its white-marbled leaves, the pot marigold mix *Calendula* 'Fiesta Gitana' or *Brachycome iberidifolia* 'Summer Skies', which produces a profusion of blue, purple and white daisies all summer. Several pansies are now available in appropriately old-fashioned pastel shades. Try *Viola* 'Watercolours' or 'Romeo and Juliet'.

4 *Arrange the longest trails of ivy to create a rim of greenery that spills out over the basket's dipped edge. Make the composition asymmetric.*

1 *Line the basket with black plastic to prevent drips if used indoors, and to protect the wicker. To make trimming the edge easier, put a quantity of gravel in the base first to keep it in place.*

2 *Add more gravel or bits of broken styrofoam plant trays to create a drainage reservoir to prevent overwatering.*

3 *For seasonal arrangements indoors and out, use a peat-based potting mix. For border perennials and alpines, use a soil-based mixture or add coarse grit to the potting mix.*

With a wide handle like this, use a butcher's hook to suspend the basket from the chain.

Campanula carpatica 'Blue Clips'

5 Fill the center of the basket with the campanulas. Try not to hide the handle, as this is very much part of the overall design. Fill any gaps with soil and firm in lightly.

7 Water the basket and hang it in a cool, well-lit spot indoors, such as a conservatory or large glass porch. Pick off dead blooms regularly, and after flowering, harden off the campanulas and plant them in the garden.

This Hedera helix *cultivar (a variegated ivy) combines well with the blue of the bellflower and stands out against the dark-colored wicker.*

6 Break off chunks of rooted ivy cuttings and use these to fill in any gaps that remain around the edge of the basket.

Fragrant jasmine in a black wire basket

There need only be a few flowers open for you to detect the presence of jasmine. The perfume is intoxicating and a single plant in full flower can fill a large room with fragrance. Jasmine makes a wonderful basket plant because of its graceful trailing habit and delicate foliage and flower clusters, but it is vigorous and will ultimately need replanting into a large pot or conservatory border.

In garden centers, you will often see indoor climbers and lax shrubs trained round hoops. This is just a way of presenting the plant tidily and is not necessary for its cultivation. Following on from the spring-flowering jasmine, you will find summer-flowering climbers, such as the passion flower *(Passiflora caerulea)*, Cape leadwort *(Plumbago auriculata)*, *Abutilon* hybrids and black-eyed Susan *(Thunbergia alata)*. All of these can be replanted to become unusual and eye-catching subjects for hanging baskets. The delicate black-eyed Susan combines well with other plants (see page 146), but the others are best planted singly in large baskets, and, like the jasmine, transferred to more conventional containers at the end of the season. The wirework basket for this project was chosen for its elegant lines and emphasizes the romantic feel created by the jasmine's airy trails.

1 Gently pull out the wire hoop and begin to untangle the stems. This can be a slow and fiddly process, but should not be hurried.

2 Although you could line this basket with plastic, you can achieve the most attractive effect with moist sphagnum moss. Mist spray the moss regularly to keep it fresh.

3 Pack the moss lining in tightly to make a thick dense layer that prevents the potting mix drying out too quickly or washing out through gaps when the basket is watered.

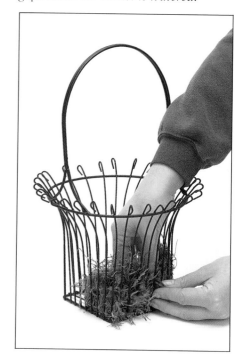

4 Add a little potting mixture to the fully lined basket. A special hanging basket mix would be ideal, as water will tend to be lost more rapidly than normal through the basket sides. Plant, filling in the gaps with more potting mix.

Jasminum polyanthum

7 Hang the finished basket in a well-lit position. Remove individual flowers as they fade, using a sharp pair of nail scissors. Water by plunging the basket in a bucket or bowl of tepid water. This will also rewet the moss.

5 Spread out the trailing jasmine stems so that they hang evenly over the sides of the basket. Then take one or two of the longest trails and wind them carefully round to cover the handle of the basket.

6 To persuade the stems to trail down in the desired position, fix them in place using long 'pins' made from bent florist's wire. Push the pins through the sphagnum moss.

109

Painting pots for a weathered look

Nowadays, you can obtain a wide range of plastic terracotta-effect pots. These have the advantage of being unbreakable, frost-proof and lightweight. Some are more realistic than others, but all have a rather raw, brand new look about them. Over a period of time, real terracotta weathers and takes on the patina of age. White salt deposits work through to the surface and in damp, shady conditions, a coating of green algae often appears. Using a variety of simple paint techniques, it is possible to mimic this transformation and achieve a realistic effect on plastic containers. Pots and planters with a high relief are the most convincing when painted, as the dark and light shading emphasizes the contours. Acrylic paint, mixed and thinned with water, is an ideal medium for this technique as it remains wet and soluble for long enough to work on and correct any mistakes, but then dries to form an effective waterproof plastic coating.

1 Mix up a small quantity of white, yellow and dark green artist's acrylic paints, adding water until the mixture becomes quite thin and runny. Tilt the wallbasket back slightly and apply the first coat.

2 Cover the face with a liberal quantity of paint. You need not be too particular at this stage and you will notice that the color tends to run off the raised portions and collect in the grooves.

3 If the color is too opaque and the terracotta does not start to show through after a couple of minutes, use a clean, wet brush and go over the raised portions of the face again, diluting the paint.

4 Use a piece of absorbent kitchen towel, scrunched up into a pad and dampened slightly, to dab off some of the paint from raised parts of the face. Do this in irregular patches.

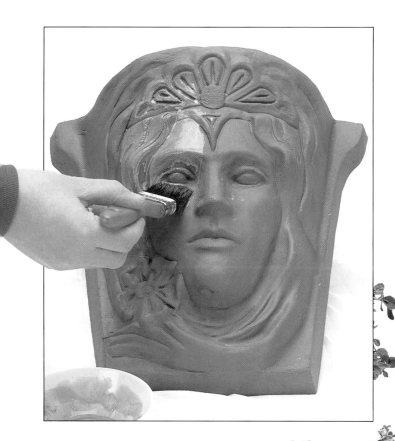

Plecostachys
serpyllifolia

Argyranthemum
frutescens *(marguerite)*

5 Once dry, apply a second coat. Adjust the mix if the first coat was too dark or light. In this case, extra white and yellow were added.

6 The paint runs down in streaks, much like weathering caused by damp conditions. Pigments separate out, adding to the illusion of age.

Create a sense of mystery in the garden by half hiding the face on a wall or fence covered in foliage. Trim plants to keep them in proportion with the head and remove dead blooms.

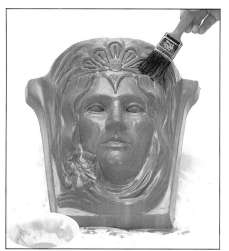

7 When dry, mix up some dark green paint and water. Using a damp, natural sponge, dab over the surface and work paint into the crevices of the face.

8 When dry, plant up the head with flowers and foliage to enhance the weathered face. Soft, old-fashioned and 'neutral' colors work well.

111

A character wall pot with ivy hair

A wall pot decorated with a carved face adds a theatrical touch to the garden. These ancient craggy features and untamed beard merely needed some wild locks to frame them and what better plant to choose than trailing ivy? Other 'hair' alternatives include the evergreen grasses and grasslike plants, such as *Carex* species and varieties - try 'Snowline' or 'Evergold' - and the blue-leaved fescues *(Festuca)*. Whatever you use, keep the planting of such pots as simple as possible to highlight rather than compete with the decoration. Double the dramatic effect by using two identical pots on either side of a doorway or, for a classical look, try mounting a single head at the top of a trellis 'pillar' to provide a focus for a bare piece of wall. Wall pots are often made from terracotta or cast cement, which looks like carved stone. They are usually quite small, with room for just a few plants and because they only hold a limited volume of soil, plants tend to dry out quickly. Pick the largest possible container and line unglazed terracotta with plastic to prevent excessive water loss through the sides. Choose plants that withstand occasional drying out - succulents and silver-leaved plants are ideal for pots attached to a hot, sunny wall.

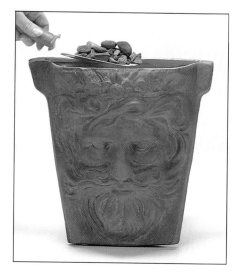

2 *Instead of drilling holes in the base of the container, fill the narrow space in the bottom section with gravel to provide drainage.*

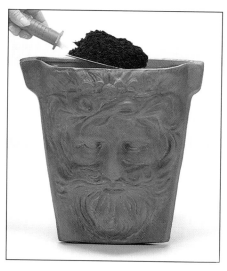

3 *Cover the gravel with potting mixture, filling the wall pot but allowing space on top for the ivies. Try one of the plants for size.*

'Meta'

'Adam'

'Golden Ester'

'Sagittifolia Variegata'

1 *Ivy is mostly used as a foil for flowers, but this blend of plain and variegated* Hedera helix *becomes a feature in its own right, creating the effect of silver-streaked hair.*

'Mini Heron'

'Goldchild'

112

A character wall pot with ivy hair

Arrange ivy trails against the wall like wisps of unruly hair.

6 Fill the gaps between the plants with more potting mixture, and water the plants. Hang the pot on two screws fixed into the wall. A sheltered, shady position is ideal to prevent damage by cold winds or scorching in strong summer sunlight.

This plastic pot has been painted to look like weathered terracotta (see page 36).

4 Squeeze the rootballs into ovals so that you can plant as many different kinds of ivy in the top as possible to make a thick head of hair.

5 Remember that the basket will be hung against a wall, so arrange some plants so that they stick up at the back.

1 *Assemble a mixture of flowering and foliage plants, with trailing and creeping varieties to cover the basket sides and bushy, upright types for the middle.*

Planting up for summer

The sooner you can plant up your summer baskets, the sooner they will start flowering. Baskets kept under glass until they are well established not only look better when hung outdoors, but also tend to be more resilient in unfavorable conditions. So, if you have a conservatory or frost-free greenhouse, you could start planting in early spring. Remember, however, that in cold areas prone to late frosts, you may have to keep baskets under cover until early summer. There is no shortage of basket plants at the very start of the season. Garden centers now sell a wide range of seedlings and rooted cuttings in small pots or 'plugs'. Some of these are perforated, allowing the roots to grow through the sides and are designed to be planted pot-and-all to lessen the shock of transplanting. These young plants are commonly referred to as 'tots'. They make planting up the sides of baskets a relatively simple affair and, unlike 'strip' bedding, plants suffer little or no root damage.

Net pots can be left in place during planting, but you must remove solid pots.

5 *Gently push the rooted cuttings through the basket sides. The neck of the plant should be just inside the wire and packed with sphagnum moss to prevent moisture loss. Cover the root-ball with more mix, filling in any gaps.*

2 *Cut out a circle of black plastic and place it in the bottom of the basket. This acts as a water reservoir and helps prevent soil loss. Add some potting mixture to hold it in place.*

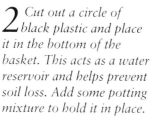

4 *Build up the sides with a thick layer of moist sphagnum moss. Pack it in tightly to prevent soil escaping when the plants are watered. Add more mix. Continue until you reach the level intended for the first row of plants.*

3 *Tuck a layer of sphagnum moss under the edge of the plastic to disguise it. Once the basket is full, you will not notice the plastic at all.*

6 Plant the large ivy, by holding the rootball horizontally and feeding the long trails through the basket sides from the inside out. Push the crown of the plant hard against the inside of the basket.

7 When the basket sides are planted up, add sufficient potting mix to cover all the exposed rootballs. Leave enough space for planting in the top.

8 Add more trailing plants to hang over the top edge of the basket. Fill in the center with upright plants, leaving room for proper development.

9 Cover the surface with a thick layer of moss. Water the basket well and hang it in a light, frost-free place until the plants are established.

10 Once young plants develop a good root system, they quickly fill out the basket. Feed them regularly to keep them flowering.

Fuchsia 'Beacon' (bush variety)

Fuchsia 'La Campanella' (cascade variety)

Verbena 'Blue Cascade'

Brachycome multifida

Hedera helix (variegated ivy)

Glechoma hederacea 'Variegata'

A shallow basket

Trugs are traditionally used for collecting cut flowers, fruit and vegetables from the garden. The attractive one in this scheme is made of thin strips of curved wood held together by a bamboo frame that adds an oriental touch. The clear, rich colors of the planting scheme complement the neutral shade of the trug, with lacquer-red picking up on the oriental theme.

New Guinea hybrid *Impatiens* are like giant-flowered versions of the ordinary busy Lizzie. The flower colors are vibrant and the long, tapering leaves are either green, bronze or brightly variegated. There are many types to choose from and all make superb, long-lasting additions to indoor displays. To keep plants compact and bushy, they need a little more light than bedding *Impatiens*, but keep them out of direct sunlight. They can be grown outdoors in summer, but perform best in a relatively warm, sheltered and humid environment, such as a lightly shaded conservatory or greenhouse. The creeping fig *(Ficus pumila)* thrives in similar conditions and its small, heart-shaped leaves and wiry, trailing habit make it a good partner for the bold *Impatiens*. The tropical red flowers seem to glow all the more strongly surrounded by pure greenery. There is a creeping fig with white-variegated foliage, but the leaves are very bright and would compete for attention in a scheme such as this.

3 *Place the first of the two Impatiens in the basket, turning it so that the stems fit round the handle. If the basket is to be viewed from one side only, you can tilt the plant to give a fuller effect.*

1 *As this is a ready-lined container, you will need to add some gravel to provide drainage. Expanded clay pellets for use in gravel trays are also suitable.*

2 *Add a layer of potting mixture. Make sure that the plants have been given a thorough soaking beforehand. Try the largest plant in the trug for size to gauge the depth of soil required.*

Use peat-based multipurpose or houseplant potting mixture.

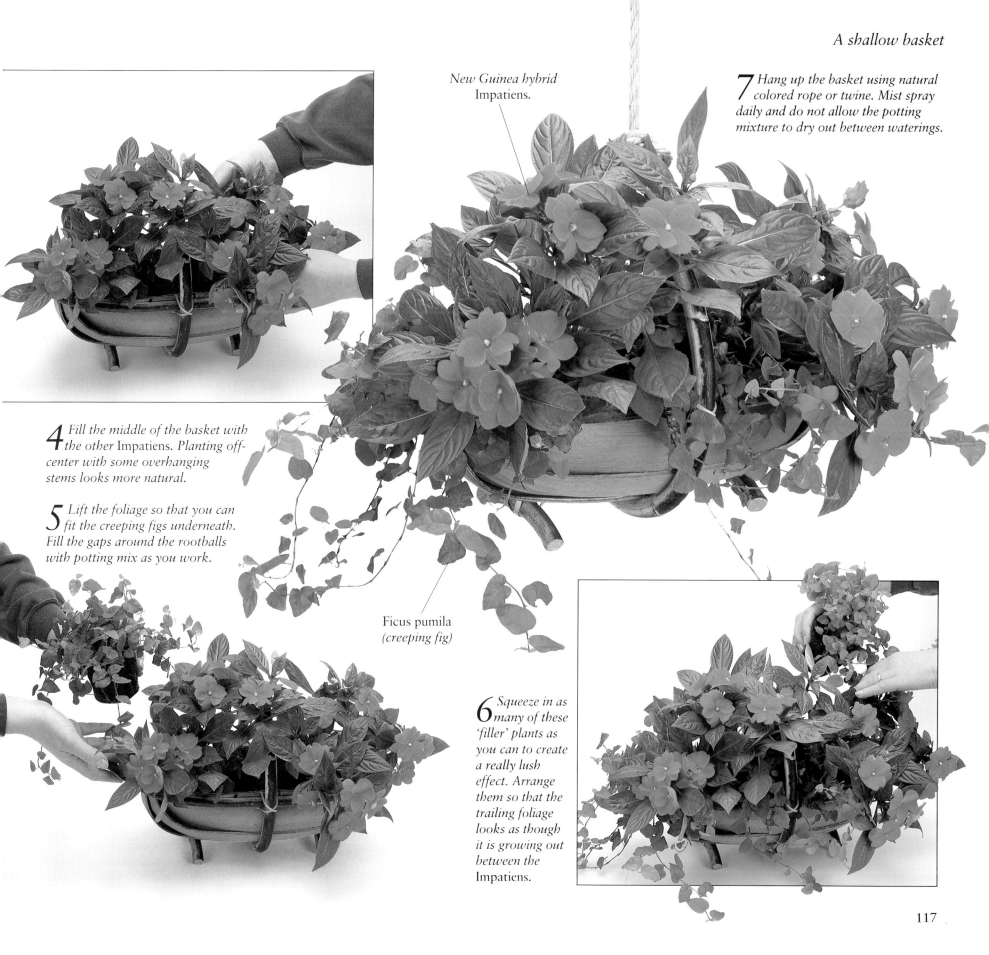

New Guinea hybrid Impatiens.

7 Hang up the basket using natural colored rope or twine. Mist spray daily and do not allow the potting mixture to dry out between waterings.

4 Fill the middle of the basket with the other Impatiens. Planting off-center with some overhanging stems looks more natural.

5 Lift the foliage so that you can fit the creeping figs underneath. Fill the gaps around the rootballs with potting mix as you work.

Ficus pumila (creeping fig)

6 Squeeze in as many of these 'filler' plants as you can to create a really lush effect. Arrange them so that the trailing foliage looks as though it is growing out between the Impatiens.

117

Red geraniums in an elegant wirework basket

Romantic, Edwardian-style wirework is back in fashion and you can now buy quite a wide range of elegant designs. The plants in this scheme were chosen to match the delicate framework. Zonal geraniums *(Pelargonium)* would have been too heavy-looking, with their solid flower heads and large rounded leaves. Ivy-leaved geraniums are far better suited; their wiry stems, covered in attractive foliage, create a much more open and airy effect. Since most baskets are viewed from below, some foliage or flower detail in the sides of the basket is essential. The brightly variegated kingfisher daisy is a good choice here, as it enjoys the same conditions as the geraniums and never gets too vigorous. Sky blue daisies sometimes appear later in the season and these would complement the rich crimson-red geranium flowers. Other suitable plants for this style of basket include tender perennials, such as the lilac blue-flowered *Brachycome multifida*, with its feathery foliage and a profusion of daisy flowers, *Argyranthemum* 'Petite Pink', a delicate dwarf marguerite with shell-pink blooms, and single fuchsias, like the red-flowered cascade variety 'Marinka'.

Above: *Wirework baskets tend to be costly; whereas ordinarily you would not mind if a basket became smothered by exuberant growth, here you will want to display at least some of the intricate decoration.*

1 Line the back and base of the basket with plastic to prevent damp seeping into the wall behind. Trim off any excess at the top or tuck it behind the frame.

2 Using thick clumps of moist sphagnum moss, begin lining the front of the basket. Tuck some between the wire and the plastic for camouflage.

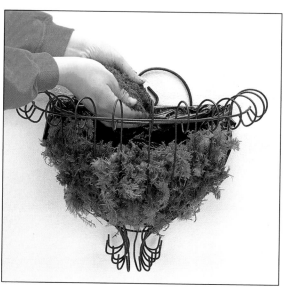

3 Firm down the moss so that it forms a solid barrier. Add potting mixture up to the point where you intend to plant through the front of the basket.

4 *Guide the shoots of the kingfisher daisies between the wires. Rest the rootball horizontally on the soil. Vary planting heights to avoid straight lines.*

5 *Fill around the plants with more moss, making sure that the neck of the plant is far enough inside the basket to avoid the risk of drying out.*

6 *Now add the first of the ivy-leaved trailing geraniums, arranging the trailing stems so that they point out to the side.*

Ivy-leaved
geranium 'Barock'

Deadhead flowers as
soon as they
start to fade.

7 *Finish planting the top of the basket, making a balanced arrangement that is wider at the top than at the base.*

8 *Fill in any gaps with soil, and water the arrangement thoroughly. Hang it up by hooking the frame over two screws fixed into a sunny wall.*

Variegated Felicia
amelloides

119

A summer basket with a purple theme

This basket contains an unusual mixture of plants in subtle shades of purple and silver-gray. The deep velvet-purple bedding viola 'Prince Henry' makes a superb contrast with the other flowers and foliage and is just right for covering the basket sides. In the top are the daisylike flowers of *Osteospermum* 'Sunny Lady', the deepest color in the 'Sunny' series. Like all osteospermums, the flowers close in shade, so hang the basket where it will receive sun for most of the day. *Nemesia fruticans* is relatively new and, perhaps surprisingly, is being marketed as a basket and container plant. The more familiar *Nemesia* is known to be intolerant of drought, but its relative certainly seems to be much more resilient, producing airy flowers all summer long. The foliage in this basket ranges from the fine, feathery leaves of *Lotus berthelotii* to the cut leaves of cineraria and the rounded, leathery, purple foliage of *Sedum* 'Bertram Anderson'. You will find this plant in the herbaceous perennial section of the garden center or nursery.

1 *Cut a piece of plastic from an old potting mixture bag and place it black-side-down in the bottom of the basket, to act as a water reservoir.*

2 *Fill the plastic 'dish' with moist, soilless potting mix. Even when the top of the basket is dry, the plant roots should find moisture here.*

3 *Using thick clumps of moist sphagnum moss, line the basket sides. Tuck moss under the edges of the plastic as camouflage.*

4 *Build up the front with bedding violas pushed horizontally through the bars. Pack in as many as will fit to create a really full display.*

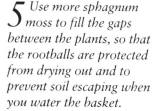

5 *Use more sphagnum moss to fill the gaps between the plants, so that the rootballs are protected from drying out and to prevent soil escaping when you water the basket.*

6 *Next add a group of cineraria, tilting one down over the basket sides to soften the edge. Pinch out the tips of these plants to keep them compact and bushy in shape.*

Osteospermum
'*Sunny Lady*'

Nemesia fruticans. *Cut
back faded flower stems to
promote further blooms.*

Sedum '*Bertram
Anderson*'

Viola '*Prince Henry*'

Senecio cineraria

Lotus berthelotii
(*coral gem*)

7 Plant the large sedum to one side
so that its long trailing shoots hang
over the edge. In mid- to late summer
it produces crimson-red flowers.

8 Plant nemesias to give height at the
back. The lotus at the front trails
over the edge; remove any orange-
red flowers that appear later on.

9 Fill in the remaining space at the
back with the osteospermum and
cover all the exposed rootballs with
potting mixture. Water thoroughly
and add more soil if gaps appear.

10 To aid moisture retention, add
a thick layer of moist sphagnum
moss over the potting mix in the top
of the basket. Allow plants to settle in
for several days by standing the basket
in a sheltered shady spot.

121

Hostas in a woodland basket for a shady place

With the exception of the variegated ivy, all the plants in this basket come from the herbaceous perennials section of the garden center. There is no reason why plants from any category - alpine, shrub, herbaceous or houseplant - cannot be used temporarily in a hanging basket, providing they are the right size with an attractive habit and long-lasting color. More drought-tolerant types are obviously better suited, as it is very difficult to keep any basket constantly moist. A number of flowering bedding plants thrive in shade, including *Fuchsia*, *Impatiens*, *Lobelia* and *Begonia*. Team them with ivies or gold-leaved foliage plants, such as the feathery golden feverfew (*Tanacetum parthenium* 'Aureum'), golden creeping Jenny (*Lysimachia nummularia* 'Aurea') or a gold-leaved hosta. Silver and gray-leaved plants do not normally tolerate shade, which is why the silver-leaved lamiums, including 'White Nancy' and 'Pink Pewter', make such useful basket plants. Some of the fernlike dicentras more often associated with woodland gardening also work well in shade. Here, 'Pearl Drops' makes a wonderful contrast with the golden hosta.

4 Add the gold-leaved hosta 'August Moon'. As well as strikingly architectural foliage, it produces pale pink bellflower spikes in midsummer.

1 There are various options for lining hanging baskets, many of which use recycled or waste materials, such as this coir matting, a by-product of the coconut industry. Wool, foam and paper are also used.

Stand the basket in the top of a large flower pot to keep it stable while you work.

2 Pour in some moisture-retentive potting mix - one designed for baskets is ideal. Here, the thick liner also protects plants from drying out.

3 Plant the dicentra, as with all plants, leaving enough of a gap at the top to allow for watering. 'Pearl Drops' goes on flowering all summer.

122

5 Plant ground-covering lamium in the rest of the basket. This variety produces a profusion of pink-hooded flowers in early and midsummer.

6 The lamium will grow out, but for instant trails, add rooted cuttings of a gold-variegated Hedera helix *variety.*

7 When the basket is full of plants, fill in any gaps with potting mix. Add a thick layer of moist sphagnum moss or fine chipped bark as a water-retaining mulch.

Hosta '*August Moon*'

Dicentra '*Pearl Drops*' has blue-gray foliage.

Hedera helix *cultivar (ivy)*

Lamium maculatum '*Pink Pewter*', a pale rose-flowered variety.

8 Hang the basket in a sheltered shaded site. At the end of the season, transfer the plants to the garden or plant them together in a wooden half barrel with some dwarf spring bulbs for a woodland effect.

123

A pink basket for cool shade

Busy Lizzies *(Impatiens)* are invaluable for baskets as they come in such a wide range of colors, from almost fluorescent reds, pinks and purples to soft pastel shades and white. There are varieties with white-striped petals, pale varieties with darker 'eyes' or picotee types, such as the one illustrated, with darker-edged petals. Single F1 hybrid bedding varieties tend to give the best performance outdoors. You can get pretty doubles, too, but these tend to be less resistant to poor weather conditions. Busy Lizzies thrive in shade but will also grow happily in full sun, although some darker-flowered varieties can bleach unless given some shelter at midday. Here, a soft pink shade has been selected to highlight the pink-splashed leaves of the variegated tradescantia. Try teaming up white-variegated apple mint or spider plants *(Chlorophytum)* with pure white impatiens or, for a more vibrant alternative, match orange, cerise-pink or red impatiens with the variegation on *Solenostemon* (coleus) leaves.

The trailing forms of tradescantia, including white-, pink- and purple-variegated, as well as plain-leaved, are popular houseplants and easy to propagate. Outdoors, grow them in sun or moderate shade, but avoid deep shade as variegated forms may revert to all-green. If you start propagating in early spring, you can have plenty of strong young plants ready for hardening off and planting in early summer. Alternatively, buy houseplant 'tots' and pot them on to promote rapid growth prior to planting. Several other houseplants perform well outdoors in summer (see panel).

3 *Plant the basket sides using bedding impatiens with a relatively small rootball, such as those sold in divided trays as opposed to pots. Push the rootball through the gaps and rest it horizontally on the soil inside.*

1 *Line the back and base of the basket with black plastic to protect the wall and prevent soil loss when watering. Camouflage with a thick layer of sphagnum moss.*

2 *Continue to line the front of the basket with moss, leaving a gap near the top to allow for planting. Fill the base with a mixture recommended for hanging baskets.*

4 Surround the neck of the plants with more moss to prevent soil leakage and to help prevent the roots from drying out. Add more impatiens in the top of the basket to soften the edges.

5 Plant a variegated tradescantia in the top and arrange the trails so that they cover the bare moss at the front. Pinch out the shoot tips occasionally to keep plants well clothed in leaves.

6 Add more tradescantias until the basket is full. Alternatively, leave a gap at the back and plant extra impatiens that will grow taller and give the display a more circular outline.

Houseplants outside

Abutilon megapotamicum 'Variegatum', Asparagus densiflorus *Sprengeri Group*, Asparagus setaceus (*syn.* A. plumosus), Begonia sutherlandii, Ceropegia woodii, Chlorophytum comosum 'Variegatum', Kalanchoe blossfeldiana, Saxifraga stolonifera, Scirpus cernuus, Soleirolia soleirolii (*formerly* Helxine), Solenostemon (Coleus), Tolmiea menziesii 'Taff's Gold', Tradescantia zebrina

Tradescantia fluminensis 'Tricolor'. Choose a bushy, compact specimen. Remove any all-green shoots that appear.

Impatiens 'Super Elfin Swirl' F1

7 Fill in any gaps with soil and water well. Hang on a shady, sheltered wall, using two screws fixed with wall plugs.

Thyme, sage and verbena

Variegated and colored-leaved herbs make attractive additions to baskets and wall planters. They often perform better than more conventional basket plants in hot, dry summers, thriving in the well-drained conditions and not minding the occasional missed watering. They also smell good, so hang them where people can gently rub the foliage and release the aromatic oils. In general, variegated herbs are not as strongly flavored as plain-leaved species, but their foliage is useful for garnishing dishes and drinks. If you are growing herbs in a basket for the kitchen, you could plant a combination of good culinary types along with more decorative varieties and add a few edible flowers, such as nasturtium, *Calendula* (pot marigold) and viola for extra color. Herbs add significantly to the range of foliage plants that you can use in baskets. For baskets in full sun, try sages, such as the all-purple *Salvia officinalis* 'Purpurascens', the pretty pink, white and purple variegated *S. o.* 'Tricolor' or the yellow-variegated *S. o.* 'Icterina'. Creeping thymes are useful all year round for covering the sides of baskets - plant bushier, more upright types in the top. There are many golden and variegated varieties to choose from and you will find them in both the herb and alpine sections of garden centers. For baskets in shade, try using one of the variegated mints, golden marjoram or the feathery leaved golden feverfew.

4 Plant the gold-variegated lemon thyme in the center of the wall pot to soften the edge. Add a variegated sage behind and slightly to one side. The sage will need pinching out to keep it bushy and in scale with the container.

1 Terracotta wall pots in sunny positions lose moisture rapidly, so always line them with plastic before planting. Cut a hole in it for drainage.

2 To ensure that the hole at the bottom does not clog up with potting mixture, add a layer of gravel or stone chippings before filling the planter with soil.

3 For a seasonal mixture of herbs and bedding plants, use a peat-based multi-purpose potting mix. For longer-term herb plantings, choose a soil-based mix.

126

5 Plant a white-flowered trailing or upright verbena in the center and another variegated sage to match the one on the opposite side. Deep cerise-pink, scarlet, purple or golden-yellow flowers would work equally well.

6 Fill in the gaps at each end with more verbenas. Most trailing types will need cutting back now and then to keep them under control. This may not be necessary with the blue-purple cascade variety, which has more delicate foliage and flower.

Salvia officinalis 'Icterina'

Verbena 'Sissinghurst White'

7 Hang the arrangement on a wall that is in sun for at least half the day. Feed and water regularly. Keep a watch for powdery mildew on the verbenas and spray them with a systemic fungicide at the first sign.

Thymus x citriodorus 'Aureus'

A spring basket

At the end of summer, dismantle the basket, removing the salvias and verbenas. You could leave the thyme in position and fill the space behind with crocus bulbs, such as Crocus chrysanthus 'Cream Beauty' or 'Zwanenburg Bronze', or gentian blue Scilla sibirica. Pack the bulbs in tightly for a good display in early spring. Or remove all the plants and replace them with blue or purple winter-flowering pansies.

127

A summer display in a manger basket

This scheme shows how easy it is to give the same container a whole new look, simply by choosing very different plants to fill it (see page 102 for alternative spring displays). Large containers such as these give far greater scope for combining plants creatively; generally speaking, the bigger the container, the more types of flower and foliage you can use to fill it, especially if you choose a fairly tight color scheme.

When selecting plants for a container, it pays to imagine what size and shape they will be after several weeks of growth. That way you will avoid the situation where one plant becomes out of proportion with the rest. This is not always easy, since information on the plant label can be rather sketchy and most young plants are of a similar size when you buy them. You will often need to trim back individual plants and it is better to begin to control vigorous types early on. For example, in the scheme featured here, you will need to pinch out the silver-leaved cinerarias occasionally to keep them bushy, as well as remove over-large leaves or shoots in the coming weeks.

1 Line the back and base of the basket with black plastic. Line the front of the basket with sphagnum moss, tucking it under the plastic.

2 Pour some potting mix into the base of the basket. Put in the first row of widely spaced Ageratum. Rest the rootballs horizontally on the soil.

3 Build up the front with pink Impatiens and more Ageratum, varying the height of the plants so that the arrangement looks more natural.

4 To stabilize plants and prevent the rootballs from drying out, pack in plenty of moist sphagnum moss around their necks. Alternatively, line the whole of the front with plastic and cut holes in it for the plants.

5 Add more potting mix to cover the rootballs, making sure that it is well worked in between the plants to avoid leaving air pockets.

6 *Plant three zonal geraniums at the back. Look for plants labelled C.V.I. (Culture Virus Indexed), which have more flowers of a better size and color.*

8 *Add F1 hybrid petunias between the geraniums and cineraria. These floribunda types are compact, free-flowering and weather resistant.*

9 *Work potting mix into the gaps and cover with sphagnum moss. Water well. Hook the basket onto a sunny wall with two large protruding screws.*

Petunia *(F1 hybrid 'Mirage Series')*

Pelargonium *(F1 hybrid PAC 'Fox')*

Senecio cineraria

7 *Plant a row of cut-leaved cinerarias at the front for a splash of silver and to provide strong textural contrast. Tilt them forward to cover the basket edge.*

Impatiens *(F1 hybrid 'Novette Series')*

Ageratum *(F1 hybrid 'Blue Danube')*

129

A classic white arrangement

If you seek to create a feeling of tranquillity and purity in your garden, consider how restful a combination of white, gray, silver and green foliage can be. However, for any monochrome scheme to be truly successful, it is important to have plenty of textural contrast between the different elements. In the basket featured here, the large, solid flower heads of petunia are planted alongside the smaller-flowered busy Lizzie and the busy Lizzie is in turn set against the froth of white alyssum. Foliage is no less important. The ferny, gray-leaved lotus has a totally different feel to the trailing ivy and both make a good contrast with the large, rounded leaves of the geranium. Bear in mind that there is a noticeable variation in the color of white flowers. Those in the basket are pure white and work well together, but the results would not have been so successful if it combined creamy whites and pure whites. Adding tiny amounts of an entirely different color will often lift an all-white scheme and make the flowers stand out all the more. Try adding the cream-variegated form of the blue, daisy-flowered *Felicia amelloides* to a creamy-white scheme or add warmth with the trailing geranium 'L'Elégante, whose variegated leaves and flowers are flushed pink. There are several other good white-variegated basket plants to choose from, including the aromatic and drought-resistant *Plectranthus coleoides* 'Marginatus', trailing nepeta or variegated ground ivy (*Glechoma hederacea* 'Variegata') and the variegated succulent trailer *Sedum lineare* 'Variegatum'. For gray and silver, choose from *Helichrysum petiolare*, *Senecio cineraria* and *Cerastium tomentosum*.

1 Stand the basket on a bucket for stability. Cut a circle from an old potting mix bag and place it black side down in the base of the basket. Fill the plastic circle with potting mix.

2 The plastic acts as a reservoir for the plants, trapping water and preventing soil from washing through. Tuck sphagnum moss under the edges for camouflage.

3 Cover the basket sides with the sweetly scented white alyssum, feeding the rootballs through the gaps to rest horizontally on the soil.

4 Pack moss around the necks of the plants to protect them from drying out. Angle the busy Lizzie so that it covers the rim of the basket.

5 *Plant a pot of the ferny* Lotus berthelotii *to trail over the edge. Next, begin planting petunias into the top and sides of the basket.*

6 *Continue to build up the basket sides with moss and plants and work soil in around the rootballs. Next add a trailing ivy.*

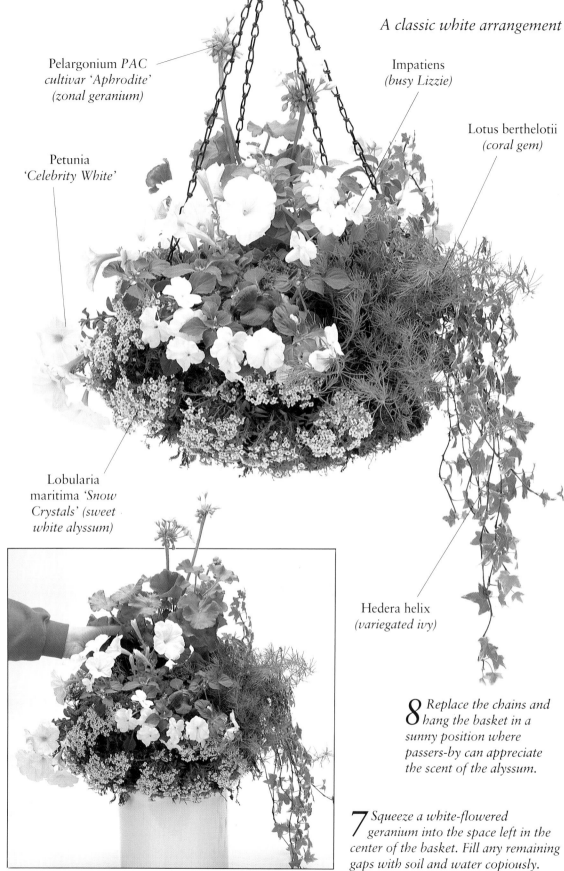

A classic white arrangement

Pelargonium *PAC cultivar 'Aphrodite' (zonal geranium)*

Impatiens *(busy Lizzie)*

Petunia *'Celebrity White'*

Lotus berthelotii *(coral gem)*

Lobularia maritima 'Snow Crystals' (sweet white alyssum)

Hedera helix *(variegated ivy)*

8 *Replace the chains and hang the basket in a sunny position where passers-by can appreciate the scent of the alyssum.*

7 *Squeeze a white-flowered geranium into the space left in the center of the basket. Fill any remaining gaps with soil and water copiously.*

131

A romantic wall basket

1 *Line the back of the basket with plastic cut from an old potting mix bag. Turn up a lip at the base to act as a water reservoir.*

Tissue paper begonias and airy asparagus fern give this wall basket the feel of a bouquet of flowers, and the rose-pink color scheme adds to the air of romance. This is a display for a site sheltered from wind and the bleaching effect of strong sunlight, where the luxuriant foliage and flowers can continue to grow unscathed. The large-leaved tuberous begonias are normally sold singly, in flower, making it easy to choose just the right shade. The F1 hybrid variety 'Non-Stop' is always a good choice and widely available, but it requires a little attention if it is to put on a really good show. The main task is to remove the two single female flowers with their winged seedpods that lie on either side of the central male flower. This will help the plant to produce much larger and more showy double flowers. Also remove dead flowers and leaves regularly to reduce the risk of botrytis (gray mold).

Since hanging baskets are nearly always attached to the walls of a house, it follows that planting schemes should blend with or emphasize the architecture around them. This basket would work well on an elegant period-style building, but might look out of place on the walls of an ultramodern town house. Choose a scheme that picks up colors used in and around the house and garden, say, the color of a front door, garden gate, shutters, wooden cladding or trellis. Orange-red brickwork can make a difficult backdrop for baskets, especially those with pink flowers. The 'safe' answer is to pick schemes containing 'neutral' silvers, grays and white, blues and purples, but baskets can be even more eye-catching featuring flame reds, oranges and touches of cream or planted with golden-yellow flowers and bronze-purple, blue-gray and silver foliage.

2 *Line the front of the basket with a thick layer of moist sphagnum moss, packing it tightly to avoid losing potting mixture through the bars.*

3 *Turning the plant on its side, feed the stems of the lamium carefully through the bars so that it covers the front of the basket.*

4 *Add potting mix to support and cover the rootball, then continue to build up the moss lining across the front and sides of the basket.*

5 *Split up a tray of bedding begonias and feed plants through the bars to fill in around the lamium stems. The plants will soon spread to cover the moss.*

6 *Add an asparagus fern. (Harden this off outdoors in advance.) Leave a gap at the front for more bedding begonias. Trim off any sections of leaf that bleach or lose their needles.*

7 *Fill in any spaces in the basket with more bedding begonias. Add the large-flowered begonias and then add sufficient soil and sphagnum moss to cover plant roots.*

Asparagus setaceus *(Asparagus fern) - not a fern at all but a relative of the lily.*

Begonia x tuberhybrida *(tuberous-rooted begonia)*

Begonia *x* tuberhybrida

Begonia semperflorens *'Olympia Pink' F1 (fibrous-rooted, or bedding begonias)*

8 *Water the basket well and do not allow it to dry out. The basket soon fills out; trim the lamium to keep it bushy. You can overwinter the fleshy begonia tubers in a frost-free place and bring the asparagus fern indoors as a houseplant.*

Lamium maculatum *'Pink Pearls' (deadnettle) - a hardy herbaceous ground cover plant.*

A wall basket of portulacas for a hot sunny spot

Vibrantly colored portulacas are the perfect choice for this little Mexican-style wall pot. These succulents thrive in a sun-baked position; in shade or if the sun goes in, they close up their flowers. Other sun worshippers that behave in the same way are the daisy-flowered osteospermums, gazanias, arctotis and the Livingstone daisy *(Dorotheanthus bellidiformis* syn. *Mesembryanthemum criniflorum).* The latter would be a good substitute for the portulaca, with its drought-resistant fleshy leaves and low, trailing habit. Deadhead it regularly, otherwise the plants go to seed and stop flowering. Portulacas tend to be sold in midsummer as mature plants in flower. Pots often contain a blend of different shades, which gives a very rich effect. The flowers are grouped in tight clusters at the shoot tips. It is quite difficult to remove spent flowers individually without damaging the buds, so wait until the whole cluster has flowered and then cut the stem back to a side shoot. Take care not to overwater succulent plants such as these; it is better to let them dry out slightly between waterings than to keep them constantly moist. For this reason, if you want to mix portulacas with other foliage, choose similarly drought-resistant types, including helichrysum, *Senecio cineraria,* sedum, sempervivum, *Festuca glauca,* geraniums, *Plecostachys* and *Lotus berthelotii.*

Fitting in plants

If you squeeze the rootball of a potgrown plant into a flattened oval without damaging the roots, you can pack more plants into the same space and achieve a greater concentration of color. Give the plants a good soaking.

1 Ensure adequate drainage by filling the base of the pot with gravel. This also helps to prevent the drainage hole from clogging with soil.

2 Use a soil-based potting mix with extra grit if necessary. Peat-based types do not drain as freely and if they dry out, are very difficult to rewet.

3 Try the first plant in the pot and adjust the soil level as necessary. Tilt the rootball slightly so that the arching stems hang over the side of the pot to create a pleasing shape.

Portulaca grandiflora

4 Add the central plant, again tilting it so that the stems hang down over the front of the pot. Leave room at the back for another plant to go in.

6 Add the final plant at the back of the pot and fill any remaining gaps with soil. Hang the pot where it will receive sunshine for most of the day.

Make sure that wall pots, especially glazed ones, have adequate drainage, as excess moisture cannot escape through the sides as it does in plain terracotta.

5 Balance the shape of the wall basket by adding a third plant on the left-hand side.

Grass and succulents in a terracotta wall pot

This simply decorated terracotta wall pot has a strong Mediterranean feel. Planting schemes invariably work best when the flowers and foliage complement the container, and here sunloving succulents and the steely blue grass *Festuca glauca* fit perfectly. There are many different varieties of *Sempervivum* (houseleek) with fleshy rosettes in various colors, from almost white to dark purple-red. They would not normally be considered for basket planting, but at the front of a small pot like this, their architectural form can be properly appreciated. An alternative group of succulents with similar looks are the frost-tender echeverias. *Echeveria secunda* var. *glauca* has beautiful, pale blue-gray leaves and contrasting spikes of yellow and red. Look for it in the houseplant section of your garden center. Flaming Katy *(Kalanchoe)* is another houseplant that is perfectly happy outdoors during the summer months once hardened off. As well as the usual orange, it is now available in shades of red, pink, yellow and white. The flower display will not last as long as traditional bedding plants, so when it is finished, replace it with other flowering succulents, such as the vibrant portulacas.

4 *Plant the houseleek at the front, tilting it slightly so that you can see the rosette clearly. Offsets will grow in due course and trail over the edge.*

1 *Cover the hole in the base with a flat stone or crock to prevent soil being washed out. Leave the pot unlined for greater drainage.*

2 *A soil-based potting mixture suits succulents well and, in the event of drying out, is easier to rewet. Fill the base and check the depth as usual.*

3 *The blue-leaved fescues provide excellent foliage contrast in baskets. They combine especially well with brilliantly colored flowers - yellows, oranges and hot reds. Being hardy and evergreen, they are also suitable for winter interest baskets; transfer them in the fall.*

Festuca glauca
(fescue)

Kalanchoe
blossfeldiana
(flaming Katy)

Sempervivum
'Feldmaier'
(houseleek)

5 *Plant the first of the kalanchoes at the back of the basket, filling in the space between the grass and the houseleek with extra soil.*

6 *Add the remaining kalanchoe, tilting it out to the side slightly to balance the shape of the basket. Alternatively, use the succulent trailer Sedum lineare 'Variegatum'.*

7 *Hook the wall pot onto two screws fixed in a bright position but out of strong midday sun, otherwise the kalanchoe flowers fade too rapidly.*

137

A cascade of white and gold

This dark green plastic wall trough makes an excellent foil for the bright lime-colored trails of creeping Jenny (*Lysimachia*) and the bushy spiraea in the center. Overall, the color scheming is quite subtle, but on a white wall, the result is cool, leafy luxuriance. The delicate white-flowered trailer, usually sold under the name *Bacopa*, is set to become an immensely popular basket and container plant. Its correct name is *Sutera cordata* 'Snowflake'. Because of its compact growth and profusion of tiny white flowers, it is an excellent 'filler' for baskets, but also makes a stunning display when planted on its own, its stems growing down to cover the basket sides completely. Trough-like wall baskets lend themselves to symmetrical planting. In a relatively short basket such as this you only need one specimen plant as a centerpiece. The pink-red flowers of the spiraea provide quite a long display, but it is the bright leaf color contrasting with the bronze-tinted new growth that is the main attraction. If you keep it well fed and watered, this basket will continue to look fresh right through into the fall, at which point the spiraea leaves develop attractive tints. Take cuttings of *Sutera* before the frosts to ensure a supply for next year and plant out the hardy lysimachia and spiraea in the garden in a slightly shaded spot to prevent leaf scorch. Cut the spiraea hard back in the spring to encourage plenty of vigorous, bright new growth.

1 Puncture the base of the trough for drainage; the spots are usually marked. Add gravel or styrofoam chips to prevent holes from clogging.

2 Add multipurpose potting mix, checking the level with the largest plant. Leave space for watering.

3 Soak the root-ball and place the spiraea in the center of the trough. Soaking plants is vital, as dry rootballs rarely manage to draw up enough moisture from the surrounding soil once planted.

4 Add more potting mix to raise the level around the spiraea, then add pots of the gold-leaved creeping Jenny. This has lemon-yellow flowers in early and midsummer.

5 Fill the remaining gaps with Sutera. *As well as white-flowered plants, the gold foliage in this basket would also look good with blue or purple lobelias, cerise-pink and red fuchsias or Begonia semperflorens.*

Sutera *thrives in sun or part shade and flowers non-stop all summer.*

6 Provided the basket is fed and watered regularly, it will need little in the way of maintenance. Snip off the dead spiraea heads when flowering has finished and trim plants to shape if they grow out of proportion.

Spiraea japonica *'Magic Carpet'*

Sutera cordata *'Snowflake'*

Trailing plants

Begonia *x* tuberhybrida *varieties*
Bidens ferulifolia
Convolvulus sabatius
Fuchsia *(trailing varieties)*
Glechoma hederacea *'Variegata'*
Hedera helix *varieties*
Helichrysum petiolare
Lamium maculatum
Lobelia *(trailing varieties)*
Lotus berthelotii
Petunia *(e.g. 'Supercascade')*
Pelargonium *(ivy-leaved geranium)*
Scaevola aemula *(e.g. 'Blue Fan')*
Sedum lineare *'Variegatum'*
Thunbergia alata
Tropaeolum *(nasturtium)*
Verbena *(trailing varieties)*

Lysimachia nummularia *'Aurea'*

139

1 *Lay a sheet of recycled wool liner in the basket and press it into place, folding the fabric as necessary. Trim off the excess with sharp scissors. Flexible liners make a better fit and you can cut through them for planting.*

There are several different types of liner, often made from recycled waste products. Choose dark-colored liners, as they tend to fade into the background when you plant up the basket.

A large display of purple and yellow

The daisylike heads of *Asteriscus maritimus* create a splash of gold at the center of this basket. It is in fact a rock garden plant, normally sold under the name 'Gold Coin', but with its dense spreading habit, attractive, round-ended leaves and profusion of flowers, it makes an excellent basket plant, too. Containers planted solely with *Asteriscus* look very effective. Another 'new' plant in this scheme is *Verbena* 'Homestead Purple', a vigorous American cultivar, with wiry stems ending in large, vivid purple flower heads that contrast perfectly with the yellow and gold plants. The basket sides are camouflaged by a yellow-variegated trailing ivy. Ivy is an indispensable basket plant - tough, tolerant and available in a bewildering variety of leaf shapes and variegation. Small specimens, little more than rooted cuttings at the start of summer, rapidly grow into good-sized plants for instant effect in winter and spring baskets. Another plant to salvage from this basket and use as a center-piece for a winter arrangement is *Erica arborea* 'Albert's Gold', whose feathery foliage adds textural interest as well as color.

2 *Add potting mix. As this is a 16in (40cm) basket, use a soilless type, so that it does not get too heavy. Offer up a plant to check the depth.*

3 *Plant yellow-variegated trailing ivy in the top to cover the front and sides of the basket. Vinca minor 'Variegata' would also work.*

4 *Arrange some plants of Asteriscus so that the stems hang over the ivy and create a ring of flowers. Deadhead as flowers turn brown in the center.*

140

5 *Plant a young specimen of Erica arborea 'Albert's Gold' in the center. Do not worry about providing acid conditions; unlike many heathers, E. arborea grows on lime-rich soils in the wild.*

Erica arborea 'Albert's Gold' (tree heath)

Verbena 'Homestead Purple'

6 *Fill the space at the back with purple-flowered verbena, arranging the stems so that some trail forwards and intermingle with the Asteriscus. Dead-head to encourage further blooms.*

Asteriscus maritimus syn. A. 'Gold Coin'

7 *Fill in any gaps with potting mix and water well. Allow to drain and hang in a sunny position. Use the correct bracket for this heavy basket.*

Hedera helix *cultivar (variegated ivy)*

141

A subtropical hanging basket

The brilliant blooms of the Brazilian scarlet sage *(Salvia splendens)* give an exotic, subtropical feel to this basket of lush foliage plants. Foliage is not often considered bold enough to act as much more than a foil for flowers, but here plants such as the multicolored *Houttuynia* and gold-striped sedge take center stage. The *Houttuynia* used in this basket is *H. cordata* 'Chameleon', which needs a well-lit position to develop its coloring properly. During summer, small white flowers with a domed center sometimes appear. The variegated sedge, *Carex hachijoensis* 'Evergold', is another plant that is easy to please, provided its roots do not run short of water. The stiff, grassy foliage arching over the basket sides contrasts perfectly with the broader-leaved *Houttuynia* and *Salvia*. At the end of summer save the carex for a winter basket or plant it at the front of a border in sun or shade to add sparkle to a planting of other winter evergreens. As a dramatic black-leaved alternative to the sedge, you could use another Japanese plant, the evergreen *Ophiopogon planiscapus* 'Nigrescens'. The final element in this basket is a bronze-purple form of bugle, *Ajuga reptans* 'Atropurpurea'. Bugles are normally evergreen to semi-evergreen, depending on the variety and severity of the winter. For the most reliable purple foliage, suitable for covering the sides of a winter basket, choose the cultivar 'Braunherz'. Blue flower spikes normally appear in spring, but bonus flowers often develop later in the year. Ajugas dislike very dry conditions and grow more rapidly when watered freely.

1 *Cut a circle from an old potting mix bag and place it black-side-down in the bottom of the basket to act as a small reservoir so that the roots can still reach moisture between waterings. Camouflage the sides by lifting the plastic and packing sphagnum moss in underneath.*

2 *Fill the reservoir with a moisture-retentive potting mix. Continue to build up the sides of the basket with a thick lining of well-compacted sphagnum moss and add soil to raise the level to planting height.*

3 *Plant three salvias at the back of the basket. The scarlet bracts remain colorful long after the protruding flowers have faded, but once the main spike has gone over, remove it to make way for the shorter flowering side shoots.*

Salvia splendens
(scarlet sage)

Houttuynia cordata
'Chameleon'

Ajuga reptans
'Atropurpurea'
(purple-leaved
bugle)

Carex hachijoensis
'Evergold'
(variegated sedge)

4 *Add a couple of trailing, purple-leaved bugles to cover one side of the basket. You could also plant smaller plants between the bars.*

7 *Mulch the top of the basket with a thick layer of sphagnum moss and stand it in a sheltered spot out of direct sun for a few days to allow the plants to settle in. Then hang in full sun.*

5 *Plant the variegated sedge on the opposite side, leaving room in the middle for the Houttuynia. Soak the rootball in a bucket of water and remove any dead or damaged leaves with a pair of nail scissors before planting.*

6 *Add the final plant, tilting it slightly to display the variegated foliage. Squeeze the rootball to fit it in. Fill any gaps between plants with potting mix and add more soil if necessary to fill spaces that appear after watering.*

143

A late-season pastel display

You can plant virtually anything in a hanging basket: this arrangement uses a mixture of tender bedding plants and hardy shrubs. Baskets are traditionally made up in spring with planting that will last through the whole summer, but that restricts the range of plants that you can use and does not allow for any seasonal variation. Hypericums and hebes are two mainstays of the late summer and fall border and there are compact varieties that also make good temporary subjects for baskets. Low-growing *Hypericum* x *moserianum* 'Tricolor' is a good choice for the front, with its arching stems covered with prettily variegated foliage and buttercup-like flowers. *Hebe* 'Purple Pixie' is just one of a range of small-leaved hebes that flower during summer and fall. Compared with traditional bedding plants, its flowering season is relatively short. For a longer-lasting display, choose *Hebe* 'Autumn Glory' or 'Midsummer Beauty'. Other alternatives for the back of the basket include the blue-flowered *Caryopteris* x *clandonensis* or *Ceratostigma willmottianum*, pinky white *Abelia grandiflora*, fuchsias and bedding dahlias. For fall color at the front, try dwarf Michaelmas daisies (available potgrown from garden centers in late summer), heathers (*Calluna* and *Erica* cultivars) or the creeping *Ceratostigma plumbaginoides*.

Hidden water reservoir below the planting space.

1 *Self-watering hanging baskets all have a reservoir, so they do not need daily watering. Here, water is transported to the plant via a wick of capillary matting.*

2 *Assemble the self-watering basket according to the instructions and stand it in the top of a large, heavy plant pot for stability. Cover the base with potting mix.*

3 *Offer up the largest plant to check the soil level. There is no watering tube in this basket; excess water drains through to the reservoir for reuse.*

4 *When planting up just one side of a basket or adding a single large plant, you may find that the basket tips over. To keep it stable and level, counterbalance the weight using a half brick or stone.*

5 *Arrange the trailing sedum to hang over the right side of the basket and plant the variegated hypericum on the opposite side. Add extra sedums to fill in any gaps.*

Hebe 'Purple Pixie'

Begonia semperflorens

Hypericum *x* moserianum 'Tricolor'

Sedum lineare 'Variegatum'

6 *White Begonia semperflorens make a visual link between the sedum and hypericum and bridge the height gap between the front and rear.*

7 *This combination of gentle colors complements the pale, stone-colored basket. Hang it in a well-lit spot, sheltered from the midday sun.*

Fitting a large plant into a basket

When you tip a new plant out of its pot, you may find loose soil at the base. Before planting, shake or gently tease the excess away from the roots so that they will fit in a relatively shallow basket.

145

Dahlias in a wicker basket

This rustic wicker basket, with its soft orange and bronzy-purple coloring, has a distinctly autumnal feel. It overflows with the charming annual climber *Thunbergia alata*, commonly known as black-eyed Susan. This is very easy to raise from seed in spring and much less expensive than buying plants in flower during summer. The stems sometimes become a little congested, so some judicious thinning may be called for to emphasize the elegant trailing habit. Pick up the *Thunbergia* first and carry it around the garden center so that you can match the flower shade exactly with a pot of bedding dahlias. In late summer, garden centers are full of these plants, with their showy blooms in a wide range of colors. Bedding dahlias remain short and compact, and with a flowering period that extends well into the fall, are ideal for container planting. Before adding them to the basket, check plants carefully for slugs and earwigs. Like *Thunbergia*, dahlias need regular feeding and must not be allowed to dry out. Take off the dead flower heads as soon as they fade, as they are quite difficult to distinguish from the buds once the petals have fallen. The glossy bronze-purple foliage of the bugle *Ajuga reptans* 'Atropurpurea' makes a striking contrast with the paler *Thunbergia*, and the trailing foliage rosettes soften the sides of the basket. The more upright *Euphorbia* provides a lighter texture altogether and makes an attractive 'filler'. This is a relatively recent introduction named 'Chameleon'.

1 Line the basket with a black plastic liner. Add some gravel or styrofoam chips to provide a drainage reservoir at the base.

2 Fill the base of the basket with moistened peat-based potting mixture. Firm lightly and then offer up the first plant to see if the level is right.

3 When using plants that have filled their pots with roots, it is especially important to soak the rootball thoroughly before planting it. Submerge it in a bucket and wait until the stream of air bubbles stops.

4 You may need to weigh down the opposite side of the basket to stop it tipping over while you decide where to plant the dahlia.

Dahlias in a wicker basket

Euphorbia dulcis 'Chameleon'. The bracts develop paler red and pink tints in the fall.

Dahlia 'Dahlietta Apricot' (bedding dahlia)

5 Lift up the dahlia foliage and tuck the Ajuga in underneath, arranging the trails so that they fall over the edge of the basket.

6 Add a couple of pots of Euphorbia between the dahlia and black-eyed Susan. Take care, as all euphorbias exude a milky-white irritant sap if damaged.

Ajuga reptans 'Atropurpurea'

7 Complete the basket with more ajugas and fill in round the plants with potting mix. Hang it up in a position out of extreme midday sun, which would bleach the flowers. To complement the coloring, use a gold chain attached to the hanging hoop.

Thunbergia alata (black-eyed Susan)

147

Violas and ivy with a fuchsia for foliage

In the border, you can enhance the beauty of individual flowering plants with a suitable backdrop of foliage. Here, the same principle has been applied to highlight a mass of viola blooms. Bedding violas are available in a range of shades, including plain and bicolored varieties. Some are almost black and tend to 'disappear' in a mixed arrangement. This velvet purple variety with its paler lilac center is much more visible, but still needs to be surrounded by lighter foliage to do it justice. White variegated plants complement the flowers perfectly. The elegant fuchsia variety 'Sharpitor' used at the back of the basket is quite unlike most bedding varieties. It has very pale green leaves, edged creamy white, with slender pendent flowers of blush pink, which are most profuse in the fall. As it is frost hardy you can replant it in the border when you dismantle the display. Variegated ground ivy and real ivy provide a foil at the front. For a brighter overall effect, try lime green and gold-variegated foliage, including the gold-leaved fuchsia variety 'Genii', *Helichrysum* 'Limelight', *Salvia officinalis* 'Icterina', golden feverfew *(Tanacetum parthenium* 'Aureum', and for trails, golden creeping Jenny (see page 64) and gold-variegated ivy.

4 Soak the remaining plants before use. Add the fuchsia specimen at the back of the basket. Plant the first of the violas, leaving room for the ground ivy.

3 Separate a pot of rooted ivy cuttings and plant some between the basket wires. Pack moss around the necks to prevent drying out and loss of soil.

1 Cut a circle of black plastic from an old potting mix bag and use it to line the base of the basket. Camouflage the edges with sphagnum moss.

2 The plastic lining traps moisture and acts like a small reservoir for the plants to draw on. Fill the basket with potting mix and add more moss.

Support the basket on a pot while you work to keep it steady.

Fuchsia magellanica
molinae *'Sharpitor'*
*(variegated hardy
fuchsia)*

Bedding violas

7 Keep all the
plants well
watered and hang
the basket in a spot
out of the midday
sun to keep the
arrangement cool.
Few bedding plants
need full sun and a
little shade often
helps the blooms
to last longer.

5 Add trailing ground ivy
around the edge to
mingle with the ivy trails.
Ground ivy roots easily;
once you have one plant, you
should never need another!

6 Add the remaining
violas and fill any gaps
with potting mix. The
violas will sort themselves
out over the next few days.
Deadhead them regularly .

Glechoma hederacea
'Variegata'
(variegated ground ivy)

Hedera helix *'Mini Adam'*
(variegated ivy)

An ivy chicken basket

Planted with moss and ivy and hung by the front door, this chicken basket is sure to attract attention! Ivies with extra-small leaves are a good choice for this arrangement, as they make a dense evergreen covering without obscuring the detail of the container. The basket demonstrates a simple but very effective technique that you can apply to make other hanging shapes, including spheres, which are made by joining two ordinary wire hanging baskets together. You can either plant in the top of the basket and train foliage to cover the outside as shown here, or using small rooted cuttings, plant directly through the sides. Baskets made in this way are more tricky to keep, especially during very hot weather, as you really need to keep the moss moist if the exposed extremities are to remain green. The easiest method is to soak the basket by sitting the base in a bowl of water. The sphagnum moss acts like a wick and draws water up through the shape. You should also add water as normal in the top of the basket to ensure that the potting mixture remains moist at all times. If the arrangement is growing indoors or in a conservatory, mist spray it daily to keep it looking its best for as long as possible.

1 This unusual wire basket is actually an egg-holder bought from a kitchen equipment store. The black plastic coating really makes it stand out and also prevents rusting. The ivy variety 'Mini Adam' was chosen because of the feathery appearance of the pointed, white-edged leaves.

2 Stuff the head with moist, tightly packed sphagnum moss that will remain in position even if it shrinks slightly. Line the rest of the basket with a thick layer of well-compressed moss, leaving a hollow planting center.

3 Fill the center with a moisture-retentive, hanging basket potting mixture. Work it thoroughly into the interior space and firm it down gently.

Hedera helix 'Mini Adam'

4 Divide up the pots of ivy, separating out the individual cuttings. Plant them in the top of the basket, making a hole for each root clump with your fingers. Arrange them in a circle for even coverage when trained.

Choose pots of ivy with long trails for quick coverage.

5 Cut lengths of florist's wire into halves or thirds and bend them like hairpins. Cover the moss-filled body with ivy by pinning the trails at intervals.

6 Leave the head uncovered so that the detail is still visible. Add some extra ivy trails to emphasize the tail, hooking them through the frame.

Loose ivy trails arch down to make the tail feathers.

7 Attach a handle of fine chain to the basket so that you can hang it up using a butcher's hook. Adjust the position so that it hangs level.

A large winter display

The delicate combination of foliage and flower is just right for this classical basket. Its pale blue-green coloring is reminiscent of ice, so the planting is designed to create a frosted effect. You could choose all-white plants, but the gradation of white through to pink is even more effective. Ornamental cabbages and cut-leaved kales produce a central rosette of foliage that is either rich purple, pink, white or a combination of these colors. Here, a deep pink cabbage highlights the much paler, frilly-leaved one at the front. These cabbages tend to lose their outer leaves through the winter, but usually produce new growth at the center. Remove yellowing leaves with sharp scissors. Erratic watering and changes in the weather can cause the plants to bolt (flower prematurely), which looks rather odd as the center telescopes out. If this happens, replace them with something equally bold, say a dwarf pink-flowered bergenia, such as 'Baby Doll'. Female varieties of the evergreen *Gaultheria* are smothered with marble-like berries by mid-fall and the fruits usually last well into late winter. An ordinary peat-based potting mixture suits these ericaceous (lime-hating) plants well. Weather-resistant, winter-flowering heathers, usually varieties of *Erica carnea*, are ideal for winter baskets, flowering for several months.

1 *Turn the basket upside down and if there are no guidance marks, pinpoint the position of your drainage holes with a soft pencil or felt-tip pen. Drill holes carefully through the plastic base.*

2 *Break styrofoam seed trays into chips as a lightweight substitute for gravel drainage. Fill the tapering base of this large basket completely, otherwise it will weigh too much.*

3 *Cover the styrofoam pieces with potting mixture. Check that there is enough room for the largest of the plant rootballs, allowing space at the top for watering. Lightly firm the soil.*

4 *Plant the largest element - here a Gaultheria mucronata - at the back. Add the heather, arranging the shoots to soften the basket edge.*

A large winter display

Gaultheria mucronata (formerly Pernettya mucronata) 'White Pearl'

Erica carnea 'Springwood White' (heather)

Ornamental cabbage

Pansy Ultima series 'Pink Shades' F1

Ornamental cabbage

5 Put in the ornamental cabbages opposite the heather, leaving a gap in the center for the pansies. Tilt the heads slightly to show off the centers.

6 Fill the center with a selection of pansies of subtly different shades to draw all the elements of the basket together. Fill the gaps with soil.

7 Water and allow to drain before attaching the three chains to the basket rim. Hang in a sunny spot sheltered from wind. Water only when the soil surface dries out slightly.

153

A cheerful basket of evergreens

This cheerful basket will liven up even the darkest winter day. The scarlet primroses really sparkle and their bold yellow centers are accentuated by the golden-variegated euonymus. From the fall to early winter, you should find all the necessary ingredients for this basket at garden centers; many young shrubs in small pots are available at this time. They may seem quite expensive for a seasonal basket, but you can of course plant them out in the garden once the display is over. Instead of the golden euonymus, you could try its white-variegated counterpart 'Emerald Gaiety', evergreen herbs and hebes, such as the pink-flushed 'Red Edge' or silver-leaved *Hebe pinguifolia* 'Pagei'. Although more often associated with summer bedding displays, cineraria is reasonably hardy and it is worth potting up a few plants towards the end of summer. Cut back any long straggly shoots or flower stems to promote bushy new growth and keep them in a sunny spot for use later on. You can always find pots of ivy with long trails in the houseplant section of garden centers; outdoor ones are rarely so luxuriant. Gradually introduce the ivy to outdoor conditions and temperatures before planting it. Conifer hedge clippings make a good substitute for moss in baskets. The fresh green coloring is especially welcome in winter - it lasts for months without turning brown. Use it thickly to help insulate the basket and prevent the soil from freezing.

1 Cut a circle of plastic from an old potting mixture bag and use it black-side-down to line the base of a wire basket.

2 Add some potting mix to act as a small reservoir that helps to prevent water from draining away too rapidly.

Pliable, leafy, conifer hedge clippings make an excellent basket lining.

3 Build up the conifer lining inside the basket, tucking the foliage under the edge of the plastic circle. Weave the pieces into each other and through the basket bars.

4 Add more potting mix until you reach the point where the first plant is to go in. Offer up the euonymus and adjust the soil level.

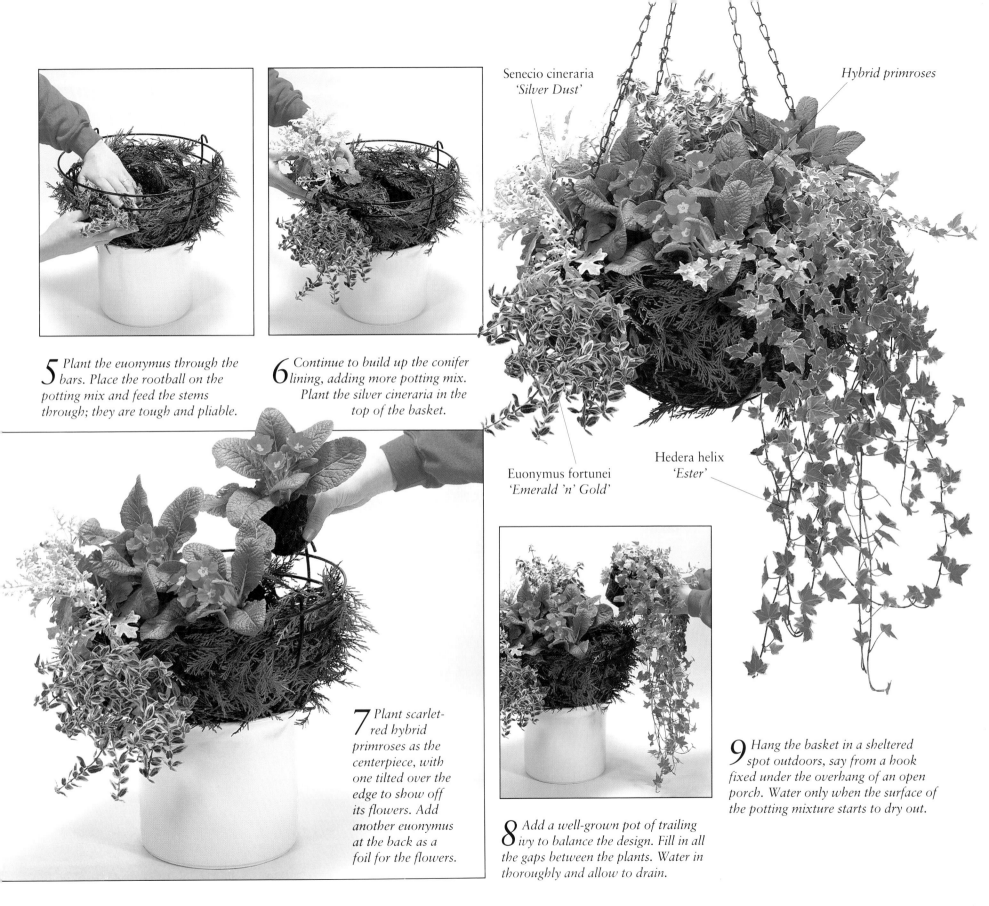

5 Plant the euonymus through the bars. Place the rootball on the potting mix and feed the stems through; they are tough and pliable.

6 Continue to build up the conifer lining, adding more potting mix. Plant the silver cineraria in the top of the basket.

7 Plant scarlet-red hybrid primroses as the centerpiece, with one tilted over the edge to show off its flowers. Add another euonymus at the back as a foil for the flowers.

8 Add a well-grown pot of trailing ivy to balance the design. Fill in all the gaps between the plants. Water in thoroughly and allow to drain.

9 Hang the basket in a sheltered spot outdoors, say from a hook fixed under the overhang of an open porch. Water only when the surface of the potting mixture starts to dry out.

Senecio cineraria 'Silver Dust'

Hybrid primroses

Euonymus fortunei 'Emerald 'n' Gold'

Hedera helix 'Ester'

155

Eye-catching pots of gold

The life of primroses can easily be extended, especially if you choose good plants in the first place. Look for compact primroses with many buds still to come and healthy, stiff dark green leaves. Gently tip the plant out of its pot to look at the root system, which should be white and well developed. Avoid plants that are pale and drawn, as these will have been kept too warm with insufficient light. Overwatering is a common problem, too. It is best to leave watering until the foliage has just started to go limp. Avoid overhead watering as this marks the foliage and flowers. Provided the basket is protected from the elements, it can be reused time and again. After the primroses, you could continue the gold theme with dwarf daffodils or little yellow violas and replace these later on with *Calceolaria* 'Sunshine' or a yellow *Kalanchoe* (flaming Katy).

1 *A simple color scheme - butter-yellow primroses and a gold chain - picks out the unusual detailing on this delightful wicker basket.*

2 *Make the basket waterproof by lining it with plastic. You can cut a circle of the appropriate size from a black bag, as here. Press the pleated lining into position inside the basket.*

3 *Carefully trim off any excess plastic until it is just below the rim of the basket so that it will be hidden by the soil. Black or clear plastic is the easiest to camouflage.*

Hardy primroses

Throughout the winter period, garden centers have tempting trays of brightly colored primroses for sale. These are normally already in flower, which makes color scheming your baskets much easier. However, be careful when buying as they are not all frost hardy - check the label or ask an assistant. Seed catalogues now offer several weather-resistant varieties, so you could grow your own supply. If you plan to grow primroses indoors, keep them in a cool, well-lit position.

8 Hang the basket in a sheltered spot. The gold chain complements the basket and the hook is made from the opened-out link of a larger chain.

4 Add a layer of gravel to provide a drainage reservoir in the base. This helps prevent overwatering, which can cause leaves to turn yellow and rot.

5 Cover the gravel with soil- or peat-based potting mixture and then test the depth by popping in one of the primroses to see the effect.

Some leaves will turn yellow as a matter of course. Remove them at the base with a pair of sharp nail scissors, along with any faded blooms.

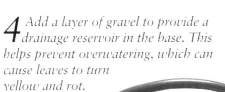

6 Plant the primroses, arranging the foliage to fit around the handle and drape over the edge. Cut off any leaves that are squashed together at the center of the arrangement.

7 Fill the gaps in between plants with more potting mixture. Firm the soil gently, making sure that there are no air pockets, as these prevent the plant roots from developing. Settle the soil in by watering, but do not overwater.

157

1 *Cut a piece of plastic sheeting to line the back of the basket and protect the wall. One corner of an empty potting mixture bag is ideal. Turn the plastic up at the base to form a lip. It may help to plant the basket in its final position to keep it stable as you work.*

A winter wall basket with berries

The festive-looking winter cherry arrives in the shops during late fall and makes an ideal subject for a basket by the front door over the holiday period. Here, pure white cyclamen, again readily available at this time of year, and white-variegated ivy provide a foil for the orange-red berries. For a richer combination, you could try scarlet-red cyclamen and dark green ivy. Although these varieties are traditionally thought of as houseplants, they will grow outdoors provided they have a sheltered, frost-free position; the warmth given out from the walls of a house and shelter from an overhead porch may be sufficient in areas where the winter is relatively mild or in the inner city.

When buying winter cherries, look for bushy plants, well-clothed in dark green leaves. There should be plenty of mostly still unripe, green berries; these will eventually turn orange. Plants like this will provide color right through until late winter.

2 *Line the front and sides of the basket with some sphagnum moss. If necessary, you can use moss salvaged from summer baskets. Use a thick, tightly packed layer to act as insulation and to prevent soil from seeping out.*

4 *Guide the trails of ivy carefully through the bars, resting the rootball on top of the soil. This arrangement uses four pots of ivy.*

3 *Add potting mixture to fill the base of the basket to just below the level of moss shown in the photograph. Break up pots of rooted ivy cuttings into manageable chunks ready for planting through the bars of the wall basket.*

5 Pack in more sphagnum moss around the neck of each clump of ivy and then continue to build up the moss lining until it reaches the top of the basket. Plant two winter cherries towards the back of the basket, leaving a gap at the front.

6 When planting the cyclamen, tilt it slightly forward so that the handsome marbled foliage hangs over the edge of the basket. Tilting the plant also helps to prevent water from collecting in the crown, which could cause the cyclamen to rot.

Solanum pseudocapsicum 'Thurino'

Cyclamen persicum

Maintenance

The plants in this basket have slightly different watering requirements. The rootball of the winter cherry should be kept constantly moist, otherwise the berries tend to drop prematurely. Ivy is quite drought-tolerant and cyclamen should be allowed to dry out slightly between waterings to prevent rotting. Do not water overhead; instead, use a watering can with a long narrow spout so that you can target the amount more accurately. Remove faded cyclamen flowers, along with any dead or yellowing leaves, with a pair of sharp nail scissors.

Hedera helix 'Hvid Kolibri'

Hedera helix 'Adam'

7 Fill the gaps between plants with more soil and cover the surface with moss to prevent erosion when watering. Water thoroughly and allow to drain.

A basket of pansies

Wicker baskets are available in all shapes and sizes. Most are unlined, but lining them is a very simple process. Since wicker is best kept under cover to prevent weathering, a wicker basket makes an ideal container for winter bedding. This also relishes the protection of an open or enclosed porch, unheated conservatory or sunroom, as it can suffer if the potting mixture freezes or when exposed to cold winds. The most widely sold winter-flowering pansies are the weather-resistant Universal and Ultima series. Most pansies can be made to flower throughout the year by sowing them at different times, so do not be surprised to see summer bedding varieties on sale in winter. As plants put on little growth until spring, choose bushy specimens with healthy dark green foliage and plenty of flower buds. Plants that show no signs of flowering are unlikely to produce blooms until spring. A basket edged in ivy can be planted up with all kinds of flowering plants, including double daisies, hybrid primroses and even dwarf bulbs, provided the container is deep enough. Keep them in a cool but sheltered place, such as a cold frame, until the bulbs are just starting to show flower buds and then bring them out on display. If you forget to buy bulbs in the fall, garden centers have a selection in pots for instant planting from midwinter.

3 *Cover the pebbles with potting mix, making sure that there is still room for the pansies and ivy on top. Check the level with a plant and adjust as necessary.*

1 *Containers with a handle convert easily to hanging baskets. This wicker basket was bought ready-lined and is ideal for use indoors, where drips may be a problem.*

2 *The sealed lining protects the basket from discoloration, but plants may become waterlogged. Add a layer of pebbles or similar material as a drainage reservoir.*

Hedera helix
'Mint Kolibri'
(ivy)

Pansy Crystal Bowl Series
'Sky Blue' F1

Add just enough water to settle the soil around the plants. Add more soil if gaps appear. Thereafter, water sparingly, allowing the soil surface to dry out slightly between waterings.

Pack the plants in tightly for maximum impact.

4 Make a continuous edging of foliage by splitting the ivy (see panel). Arrange the long trails to hang over the edges. You could also wind some pieces around the handle.

5 Plant the pansies close together in the center of the basket; they will not grow much during the winter. Fill the spaces in between with potting mix and firm in.

6 Hang the basket by a homemade rope fixed around the handle. Disguise the join with raffia. If you prefer, use a large hook and chain.

Dividing ivy

Each pot of trailing ivy probably contains seven or eight rooted cuttings around the rim. For this basket edging, simply open out the circle of cuttings into a straight line. Ivy roots easily; you can produce a winter supply by propagating it in summer. It is also available all year from garden centers.

161

Ferns in an oriental basket

The container you select will often dictate the type of foliage and flowers you choose to plant in it. This little basket looks very similar to the bamboo pots used in Chinese cooking, so a plant with an oriental feel was chosen to fill it. The foliage of the *Pteris* fern looks at first glance like that of dwarf bamboo and the pale biscuit color of the basket shows off the rich green fronds perfectly. *Pteris* ferns are some of the easiest to maintain and tolerate temperatures as low as 45°F(7°C) in winter. Like all ferns they enjoy a humid atmosphere, so hang them in the bathroom or near the kitchen sink and try to remember to mist the foliage daily with tepid water. They are ideal for brightening up a window that receives no sun at midday or for hanging in the shaded end of a conservatory. Indeed, you must keep *Pteris* out of direct sunlight otherwise the leaves may scorch. The success of this basket demonstrates the fact that you do not need a variety of plants to make a good display. Simplicity is nearly always the key to success. If you can, try to imagine your proposed plantings in black and white so that you are able to concentrate on the form of the foliage and flower as opposed to the color. That way, you can see if there is enough textural interest and overall contrast between the different elements. In the basket described here, the leaves of the fern have such a beautiful shape and shading, that there is really no need to introduce another variety.

Indoor plants with an oriental flavor

Aeschynanthus radicans (*lipstick vine*), Asparagus ferns
Foliage begonias, such as Begonia rex *hybrids*
Forest cacti (Schlumbergera *and* Rhipsalidopsis)
Clerodendrum thomsoniae
Red mini-cyclamen
Columnea *sp. (goldfish plant and varieties)*
Dwarf Cyperus *(keep moist)*
Euonymus japonicus '*Aureus*'
Ficus radicans '*Variegata*'
Red, single-flowered, trailing fuchsia, e.g. 'Marinka'
Lachenalia aloides
Maranta leuconeura erythroneura (*herringbone plant*)
Scirpus cernuus (*keep moist*)

1 *Add gravel to provide a layer of drainage in the base of the container. This basket is ready lined and has no drainage holes.*

2 *Cover the gravel with a peat-based potting mix. At this stage you can offer up a plant to check the depth and ensure that there will be a sufficient gap at the top to allow for watering.*

Pteris cretica
albolineata
*(variegated table
fern)*

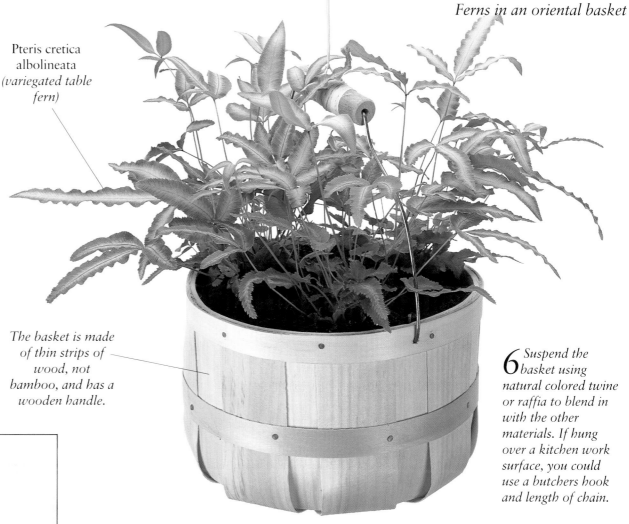

The basket is made
of thin strips of
wood, not
bamboo, and has a
wooden handle.

3 *Before putting in any plants, soak
the rootballs thoroughly. Put in the
first of the three* Pteris *ferns. Odd
numbers work better than even ones.*

6 *Suspend the
basket using
natural colored twine
or raffia to blend in
with the other
materials. If hung
over a kitchen work
surface, you could
use a butchers hook
and length of chain.*

4 *Add the remaining ferns,
adjusting their position so that
the foliage fills the basket and works
in comfortably around the handle.*

*Keep plants looking their
best by removing brown
or damaged fronds at the
base with nail scissors.
Take care not to damage
the new shoots growing
up from the base.*

5 *Fill the gaps in between with more
potting mix and firm in. Water to
settle the soil. Ferns like a constantly
moist but not wet soil, so take care
not to overwater this sealed container.*

A heather basket

The compact shape and free-flowering habit of winter-flowering heathers make them perfect for hanging baskets. Since they are well able to withstand the weather, you need not keep them in particularly sheltered situations, nor do the plants stop flowering or look battered if the weather turns nasty. In the Northern Hemisphere, there is no reason why you should not add ribbons, artificial berries, sprigs of holly, baubles or other decorations to give the container a festive touch for the Christmas period, or even illuminate it with colored outdoor fairy lights. The secret of success with any winter container is to buy evenly shaped plants just coming into flower at the start of the season and to fill it generously, as plants cannot be expected to grow and hide any gaps at that time of year.

1 Six heathers in small pots and a large variegated ivy with plenty of long trails are enough to fill a medium-sized hanging basket; this is a self-watering type for low maintenance.

3 Knock the ivy out of its pot and plant it - with its stake - so that the top of the rootball is about 0.5in (1.25cm) below the rim of the pot. Firm gently so it stands up straight.

4 Tip out the two gold-leaved heathers and plant them close together at the front of the container, Their bright foliage complements the variegated markings in the ivy leaves.

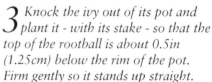

Three or five winter heathers make a good display on their own, but for more of a show add trailing variegated or frilly leaved ivy. Hang the finished basket sufficiently low so that you can see inside it.

2 Roughly half-fill the basket with any good-quality potting mixture, but do not firm it down at this stage. If you are using a self-watering basket, do not fill the reservoir until you have finished planting up the basket.

5 Use the flowering heathers to fill the sides of the basket, turning them so the shoots cascade over the edges to create the fullest possible display without swamping the smaller gold plants.

6 Using a small hand trowel, scoop a little extra potting mix into any gaps between the rootballs. This prevents the roots drying out, which could make the flowers finish early and cause the foliage to turn brown.

7 Cut the ties holding the ivy stems to the cane and untangle the 'trails' so they are all separate, ready to be arranged round the hanging basket.

Tying up the trails

Here, the trails are tied to the supporting chains. The effect is more dramatic, especially when the basket is to hang higher up and make a bold statement.

Right: Leave winter heathers in containers for one season only and then plant them in the garden in mid-spring.

8 Arrange the ivy trails around the edge of the basket and in the heather. This looks best where the inside of a low hanging basket will be easily visible.

A winter hanging basket

Given a reasonably sheltered sunny spot, it is possible to keep hanging baskets looking good all winter. Choose from the limited range of suitable flowers backed up by plenty of evergreens. The most reliable winter flowers are 'Universal' pansies and hybrid primroses. (Other winter-flowering pansies are available, but the more expensive 'Universal' strain flowers even in cold weather; hybrid primroses are like colored versions of the wild kind, and with bigger flowers - they start flowering much earlier than the rather similar polyanthus.) Add small evergreens such as ivy, euonymus, santolina or periwinkle (variegated versions are specially pretty). Use the trailing kinds around the edge for a fuller, softer effect. In big cities, the microclimate often makes it possible to grow relatively tender plants outdoors in winter; almost hardy indoor plants such as cyclamen, winter cherry, cineraria and asparagus fern often thrive. Look around the neighborhood, and if other people can grow them, go ahead. There is no need to buy special hanging baskets for winter displays; you can reuse ordinary summer ones, but avoid those with built-in drip trays or water reservoirs unless the basket is to be kept under cover - excess watering can be a problem in winter.

1 Assemble the plants, basket and potting mixture. If it has a rounded base, sit the basket in an upturned bucket to make it easier to work on. Drape the chains over the outside.

Choose variegated or frilly green kinds of ivy to contrast with the flowers.

2 Three-quarters fill the basket with potting mixture. This leaves room for the rootballs of your plants, which will virtually fill the top 3in (7.5cm) of space in the basket. Remove plants from their pots before planting.

3 Put in the plants without disturbing the rootballs. (This ensures that the flowers and buds do not receive a check in growth that could abort them.) Tuck them close together.

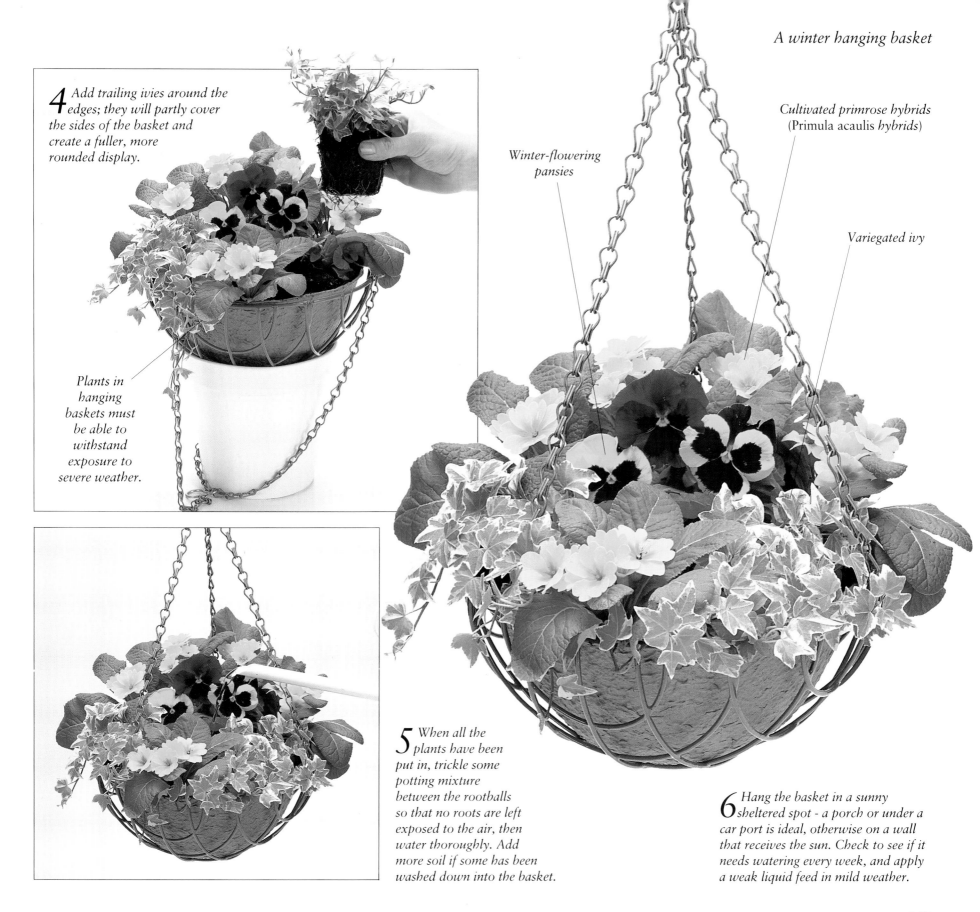

4 Add trailing ivies around the edges; they will partly cover the sides of the basket and create a fuller, more rounded display.

Plants in hanging baskets must be able to withstand exposure to severe weather.

A winter hanging basket

Winter-flowering pansies

Cultivated primrose hybrids (Primula acaulis *hybrids*)

Variegated ivy

5 When all the plants have been put in, trickle some potting mixture between the rootballs so that no roots are left exposed to the air, then water thoroughly. Add more soil if some has been washed down into the basket.

6 Hang the basket in a sunny sheltered spot - a porch or under a car port is ideal, otherwise on a wall that receives the sun. Check to see if it needs watering every week, and apply a weak liquid feed in mild weather.

Applying moldings

You can apply a range of decorative moldings, including carved beading, to smooth-sided windowboxes using waterproof wood glue. Novelty magnets and mini wall hangings could be used to similar effect. For an oriental look, try split bamboo canes, stained and finished with yacht varnish. Ceramic tiles can be applied with waterproof cement.

1 Measure and mark the position of the molding. Glue it in place and weight it down. When dry, thoroughly seal it with wood or universal primer.

2 Depending on the coverage, apply two or more coats of high gloss paint, sanding lightly between coats. Paint moldings on the flat to prevent paint dripping.

Decorating your windowboxes

It is quite easy to construct your own windowboxes using tongue-and-grooved cladding or 0.15in(4mm)-thick exterior-quality plywood. Your local supplier will often cut individual pieces to size and you need not make any fancy joints; just stick the side and base panels together using wooden strengthening struts bonded with waterproof wood adhesive and secure them with fine nails and screws. It is now possible to buy preservative wood stains in a wide range of attractive colors, including blue. If you prefer to decorate the outside of the box with paint, only use wood preservative on the inside and underneath. If it seeps through cracks to the outside, use a sealant such as aluminum paint followed by universal primer before attempting to apply the top coats, otherwise the preservative color will keep working its way through to the surface.

One of the easiest yet most striking ways of decorating a wooden windowbox is to use stencils. Many designs are available from shops or by mail order. You can buy special pots of stencil paint, but provided you use paint of a suitable consistency, you can just as easily use artist's acrylics or dilute matt emulsion - even one of the mini 'tester' pots. Another way to add a note of distinction is to use decorative wood moldings. Once firmly secured and painted, the effect is of carved wood or cast metal. Terracotta often looks very raw and orange when new. You can 'age' the surface quickly using a very dilute color-wash of artist's acrylic. As the water is absorbed into the terracotta, an uneven and natural-looking covering of white pigment remains. Apply other colors according to your chosen scheme.

Gold fleur-de-lis

1 Shake the pot to get a little paint onto the lid. Dip the stencil brush lightly into the lid. Remove excess paint on a piece of paper.

1 Using diluted white artist's acrylic paint, roughly apply a wash to the surface of the dry terracotta container. The uneven coverage or drips are all part of the distressed look.

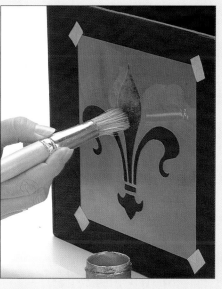

Seashell motif

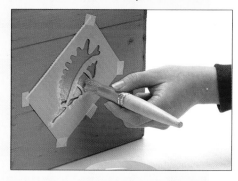

2 Keeping the brush perpendicular to the windowbox, lightly tap the paint onto the wood to give a stippled effect. Overlap the stencil as you work.

3 For more solid coverage, keep the brush in light contact with the wood, making small circular movements. Work well into the corners.

4 Applying stippled and solid paint creates light and shade and produces a three-dimensional look. It also suggests age.

1 Attach the stencil with small pieces of low-tack masking tape. Use a stencil brush and dilute artist's acrylic paints.

2 Mix your colors together, here crimson and ultramarine, with some more white paint. Apply in downward strokes to create darker and lighter 'weathered' streaks.

Below: You can paint terracotta to match any planting scheme. If you line the inside of the windowbox with plastic, the color will last longer.

2 You can also achieve a stippled look using a natural sponge. Dab excess paint onto newspaper before applying it.

A windowbox for spring

This smart red windowbox is made from tongue-and-grooved cladding, topcoated with high gloss burgundy-red paint. The predominantly red and yellow color scheme brightens up dull winter and spring days and demonstrates a useful labor-saving approach to windowboxes. This is to use a backbone planting of evergreens and simply swap over the small seasonal element - bulbs, bedding or flowering herbaceous perennials - as and when the display finishes. The daffodils used here will easily lift out to make room for summer bedding, such as yellow *Calceolaria integrifolia* 'Sunshine', Afro-French marigolds or *Coreopsis grandiflora* 'Sunray', and red nasturtiums, such as 'Empress of India', petunias, salvias or verbenas. In the fall, dwarf yellow or red dahlias would make excellent substitutes. Bulbs are especially useful for providing early seasonal color, and apart from dwarf daffodils, the following would also work well in this windowbox: deep blue hyacinths, grape hyacinths (*Muscari armeniacum* cultivars) or *Scilla siberica* and red early dwarf tulips, such as 'Red Riding Hood' or *Tulipa praestans* 'Fusilier'. Bulbs often perform best in their first year, so as soon as flowering has finished, either deadhead and lift the clumps, transferring them to the garden to finish ripening, or discard them. In the fall, select the largest grade of bulb and pot to grow in the greenhouse or cold frame over winter so that you have good, strong plants to insert in the spring, or buy potgrown plants from the garden center.

1 Choose a plastic trough to act as a liner. Construct the decorative box so that you still have room to grip the liner at each end and can remove it easily for replanting or if you need to replace it with a new liner.

2 Cover the drainage holes with plastic fine-mesh windbreak netting or metal mesh. This prevents soil clogging the holes or being lost through watering. The outer box needs drainage holes, too.

3 Add 1in(2.5cm) depth of gravel to provide drainage and help prevent the plant roots from becoming too wet. Note that the liner should also be slightly raised off the base of the box.

4 Pour in some peat- or soil-based potting mixture to cover the gravel and then add three equally spaced specimens of the gold-variegated Euonymus japonicus 'Aureus'.

5 Plant two clumps of miniature daffodils between the shrubs. The variety 'Tête à Tête' is a multiheaded type that flowers early in the season.

6 Lift a clump of blue Vinca minor from the garden or buy a well-grown plant in a 7.5in(19cm) pot and split it in half with a garden knife.

7 Fill in the gaps with gold-variegated trailing ivy. Arrange the stems so that they fall over the two ends of the box as well as the front.

Narcissus *'Tête à Tête'*

Euonymus japonicus *'Aureus' makes an excellent foil for the daffodils.*

Blue-flowered Vinca minor *has a cooling effect on the scheme.*

Hedera helix *cultivar*

8 This scheme will perform well in a sunny or moderately shady spot and needs just light trimming from time to time. Replace the daffodils once they fade.

A child's windowbox

The secret of making gardening fun for children is to find a way for them to get dramatic results for very little effort. They love to watch seeds germinate but are impatient to see the results. Hardy annuals, such as nasturtiums, candytuft (*Iberis umbellata*) and pot marigolds (*Calendula*), are ideal, since the seed is quite large and relatively easy for little fingers to handle, germination is rapid and the plants produce plenty of large bright blooms. You can raise seeds in individual pots on the windowsill and plant them in the box when they are large enough to handle or, where plants resent disturbance, such as the Californian poppy (*Eschscholzia*), sow them direct. Mixed packets of hardy annuals are also fun for children; the results may look chaotic to you, but they will love the variety. To overcome the problem of small seed and difficult germination, buy bedding as plug plants or baby plants in net pots. Children can pot the plants up separately and take care of them until they are large enough to plant out. Most of the common bulbs are also very reliable in containers. Buy a selection of dwarf and low-growing types with bright flowers that will bloom from late winter to late spring and help the children to fill the box in layers according to the planting depth stated. Cram in as many as possible for really impressive results.

4 *Plant alternate blue and yellow pansies at the base of the cat, working soil around the rootballs. Mixed French marigolds or, for shade, Mimulus 'Calypso', would also work well.*

3 *Place a topiary cat in the center of the windowbox. You can buy two-dimensional animal frames, either ready planted with ivy, (as here), or to make up yourself.*

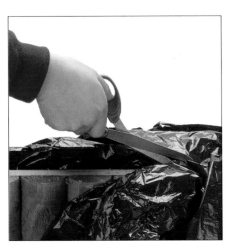

1 *This rustic windowbox is too small to take a rigid plastic liner, so to help prevent rotting, treat it with wood preservative and line with black plastic.*

2 *Cut holes in the bottom of the liner so that excess water can drain away through holes in the box. Add a layer of multipurpose potting mix.*

Hedera helix
'Sagittifolia'

Easy topiary

Simple topiary frames are quite easy to make, but you can also buy them from garden centers or by mail order. The best plants to use are small-leaved Hedera helix varieties. Wind the stems round the wire as they grow, but leave the 'features' uncovered, otherwise the outline may become unrecognizable.

5 Put in the last of the pansies then check that all the gaps round the plants have been filled with soil. Give the box a good soaking.

6 This cat figure sitting in its bed is sure to appeal to children! Remove fading flowers and stalks with sharp scissors, and feed and water regularly.

F1 hybrid pansies

Protecting the paintwork

Untreated, the stencil motif and blue 'stain' would begin to weather quite rapidly. Seal it using exterior-quality or yacht varnish, described as matt or silk/low sheen. Although colorless, the varnish will darken the paintwork slightly.

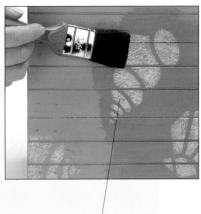

Apply two thin coats of varnish.

A seaside windowbox

This wooden box with sides reminiscent of weatherboarding has a strong seaside flavor. The wood was painted using a mini 'tester' pot of blue emulsion, diluted down so that it just colored the wood like a stain, rather than masking it completely. (For directions on how to apply the stencilled motif, see page 169.) When gardening next to the sea, select varieties that are resistant to salt-laden winds. Shrubs, herbs and grasses with silver-gray foliage are worth looking out for because they often perform well in this environment. Their coloring results from the foliage and stems being covered in light-reflective hairs, or wool, which protect the plant from rapid moisture loss. Succulents and plants with small, glossy leaves, such as *Euonymus*, hebe and dwarf cotoneaster, also do well. During summer, hebe, lavender, *Brachyglottis* and cotton lavender (*Santolina*) will all flower, adding white, blue and yellow to the scheme. For extra spring color, you could interplant with one of the dwarf early *Crocus chrysanthus* varieties, *Scilla siberica* or a dwarf iris such as *Iris histrioides* 'Major' or the variety 'Harmony', all of which would look well against a gravel mulch and silver-gray foliage backdrop.

1 *Good drainage is imperative for silver-leaved plants and herbs. Cover the drainage holes in the base of the liner with fine plastic mesh to prevent soil from clogging them up or being washed away through to the outer cover.*

2 *Add about 2.5cm(1in) depth of gravel over the mesh. This will also help to filter out soil particles from the drainage water as well as preventing waterlogging. You could also use styrofoam packaging chips.*

3 *Before planting, arrange the shrubs on the ground to find the best combination. Put the Brachyglottis in the center; add the euonymus to soften the hard edge.*

4 *Plant the cotton lavender in the back corner. Try to avoid planting in a straight line, as this does not look natural. Add the low-growing hebe.*

Brachyglottis *Dunedin Hybrids Group 'Sunshine' (syn* Senecio *'Sunshine')*

5 *Finally add a lavender. Work the soil round the root balls to avoid air pockets. Use a soil-based potting mix with extra grit for good drainage.*

Hebe pinguifolia *'Pagei'*

Lavandula *x* intermedia *Dutch Group. This is a compact, busy lavender specimen.*

Euonymus fortunei *'Emerald Gaiety' (variegated euonymus)*

Santolina chamaecyparissus *(cotton lavender)*

6 *Add a decorative mulch of gold-colored gravel to set off the plants and to prevent water and soil splashing up onto the stems and lower leaves, which might lead to rotting.*

7 *Fix up the windowbox in full sun. Trim the lavender lightly after flowering. The hebe should not need attention. Prune other plants hard back if necessary in spring.*

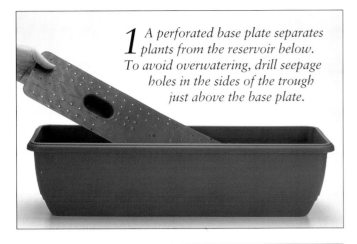

1 *A perforated base plate separates plants from the reservoir below. To avoid overwatering, drill seepage holes in the sides of the trough just above the base plate.*

2 *Cover the base plate with a layer of soil-based potting mixture. For drought-resistant plants and herbs, add extra grit.*

Summer flowers and herbs in a trough

Most herbs are drought tolerant and make excellent subjects for containers, especially if you forget to water regularly. There are many attractive foliage forms with colored or variegated leaves, as well as plants with attractive flowers, and most combine easily with flowering bedding plants and tender perennials. In this windowbox, an interesting mix of textures has been created by blending the rounded shapes of the geranium and pansy with the feathery upright shoots of rosemary and low mounds of golden oregano. Other shrubby herbs that would provide an attractive foil for flowers include lavender, hyssop, curry plant (*Helichrysum italicum* - its leaves smell strongly of curry!), cotton lavender (*Santolina chamaecyparissus*), several of the silver-leaved artemisias and sage, especially the highly ornamental *Salvia officinalis* 'Icterina', which has gold variegation, and the purple sage (*S.o.* 'Purpurea'). Low-growing alternatives to oregano for the front of the box might include double-flowered chamomile (*Chamaemelum nobile* var. *flore-pleno*), with its creamy pompon flowers and feathery foliage that smells sweet and fruity when disturbed, or the golden, creeping lemon thyme (*Thymus* x *citriodorus* 'Aureus') which, as its name suggests, has the pungent aroma of lemons.

3 *Plant a row of geraniums at the back and interplant with young, vigorous rosemary plants. If growth is thin, trim the shoot tips to encourage bushiness.*

4 *To soften the front edge, plant five equally spaced golden oreganos. Gently squeeze the rootball into an oval to allow more room for the pansies.*

Soaking rootballs

Rootballs must be thoroughly moist before planting. Plunge the pot into a bucket, below the water surface. When the stream of bubbles stops, remove the pot and set it aside to drain.

5 Add sparkle to the display with some cream-colored blooms. Fill the gaps between the plants, both at the front and back of the box, with as many pansies as possible.

6 Choose a brightly lit situation for this planting. Feed and water it regularly, but take care not to let the soil become too wet. Remove dead heads and flower stems and pinch back rosemary shoot tips to keep the growth compact.

Origanum vulgare 'Aureum'

Pansy F1 hybrid

Geranium Century Series Orchid F1

Rosmarinus officinalis 'Miss Jessopp's Upright'

1 *Protect wooden containers from rot caused by contact with damp soil by using a rigid plastic inner liner. There should be enough room to grip the ends of the box with your fingers for easy removal.*

A Gothic-style windowbox

Heraldic lilies, otherwise known as fleur-de-lis, and medieval stars adorn this wooden windowbox. It would look well on an older facade, but the beauty of stencils is that you can use different motifs to emphasize whatever mood and visual style you have chosen for your house and garden. To achieve the patina of age, roughly brush over the windowbox with artist's acrylic paint - here in a shade appropriately called Monestial Blue - and apply the antique gold paint unevenly to make it appear worn (see also page 169). The planting was also chosen to be reminiscent of olden days - roses, double primroses and ivy all have a long history as garden plants. You would not normally see roses flowering at the same time as primroses, but in spring the houseplant sections of garden centers often have miniature roses that have been forced into bloom early. These much prefer to be grown in a cool, airy situation and can be acclimatized to outdoor conditions quite quickly if given frost protection.

2 *Cover the holes in the liner with a piece of fine plastic mesh to prevent soil loss and stop leakage into the base of the wooden surround. You can tape small pieces of mesh over individual holes before adding the gravel.*

3 *The outer decorative cover only needs to be about 0.4in(1cm) higher than the liner to hide it from view when planted up. Ensure good drainage by pouring in a layer of gravel or styrofoam packaging chips.*

4 *Fill the back of the windowbox with miniature roses. Feed with a liquid fertilizer designed for flowering plants and remove dead heads regularly.*

6 Fill the gaps between the primroses with a compact, small-leaved ivy. Trim back long trails to avoid obscuring the design. If you want a flowering cascade for summer, pick something delicate, such as blue trailing verbena or lobelia.

5 Plant a row of equally spaced double primroses along the front. When they finish flowering, replace them with something suitable, such as double red busy lizzies.

Primula 'Miss Indigo'
(double hardy
primrose)

Miniature rose

Hedera helix
cultivar
(variegated ivy)

7 Regularly remove fading flower heads and yellowing leaves from the primroses. Use secateurs to deadhead the roses. Feed and water the box regularly and watch for aphids.

179

A terracotta windowbox

1 *Cover each of the large drainage holes in the terracotta windowbox with a clay crock to prevent soil from being washed out during watering.*

2 *Add gravel for drainage, particularly if you are lining a terracotta container with plastic to prevent moisture loss through the sides.*

Painting terracotta may seem rather unconventional, but an effect like this is very easy to achieve (see page 168). As an alternative colorway, try a mint-green base coat sponged over lightly with white to give a mottled effect and fill the windowbox with soft apricot tuberous begonias, fuchsias and busy Lizzies in shades of pink, peach and white, all with a foil of white-variegated foliage. A rich powder-blue would suit the strong orange and lemon shades found in a pot marigold mix such as *Calendula* 'Fiesta Gitana', or mixed nasturtiums such as 'Alaska'. Alternatively, use a mid purple-blue as a base coat and add touches of crimson, blue and white paint diluted with water to the relief pattern. Plant with deep purple, velvet red and light lavender-blue flowers and silver foliage. For example, at the back you might use *Salvia farinacea* 'Victoria' and in the foreground crimson-red verbena and deep purple petunia, interplanted with silver cut-leaved cineraria and red trailing lobelia. Highly ornate terracotta windowboxes are perfect for a period setting, but if you plant with modern-looking bedding varieties, you could spoil the illusion of age. Look out for soft, subtle and muted shades; pansies such as *Viola* 'Imperial Antique Shades' and 'Watercolours', *Verbena* 'Peaches and Cream' and *Nicotiana* 'Havana Apple-blossom'. And do not forget the many herbs, small-flowered bedding violas, *Erigeron karvinskianus* 'Profusion', marguerites, heliotrope and scented-leaf geraniums.

3 *Use a peat-based potting mix for most summer bedding. For shrubs, herbs and long-term plantings, use a soil-based mix and for nasturtiums a soil-based seed and cuttings mix.*

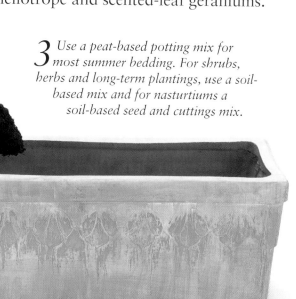

4 *Impatiens are available in a wide range of colors. Pick a shade that tones with or complements the color of the container. Here a blush-pink busy Lizzie with a dark eye is teamed up with a deeper pink one.*

5 In keeping with the pastel scheme, interplant the front row of Impatiens with a white-variegated ivy. As an alternative, use the delicate white-flowered trailer Sutera cordata 'Snowflake' or white lobelia.

6 This deep pink busy Lizzie picks up on the dark eye of the paler flower. Use it to fill in the gaps at the back, then work in more soil around each of the plants so that the rootballs are properly covered.

7 This pretty pastel display is perfect for lightening shady walls. Other summer interest plants to consider in this situation include bedding fuchsias, tuberous and fibrous-rooted begonias, violas and Lamium maculatum 'White Nancy'.

Buying bedding Impatiens in single shades makes for easier color scheming.

Hedera helix *cultivar. You can choose from a very wide range of ivies to suit a variety of planting schemes.*

F1 *hybrid* Impatiens *are more expensive than open-pollinated kinds, but usually perform better under a range of conditions.*

1 To protect the wooden cover and for easy maintenance, use a rigid plastic trough as a liner. Cover the drainage holes with fine-mesh netting to prevent soil escaping during watering.

2 Add 1in(2.5cm) of gravel as a drainage layer, to keep the soil in place and prevent clogging of the drainage holes. Sharp drainage is vital for drought-tolerant plants.

A Victorian-style windowbox

You could be fooled into thinking that this windowbox was an example of Victorian cast-ironwork. For details of how to achieve the look using wooden moldings, see page 168. If you have a formal garden, then symmetry and architectural form will feature strongly. In this case, a traditional topiary shape has been used as the central focus. Clipped geometric shapes, such as cones, spirals, pyramids and ball-headed standards, would also work well, but the sphere is the easiest shape to clip if you are new to the art of topiary. Dwarf box *(Buxus sempervirens* 'Suffruticosa') is ideal, as the foliage is fine and densely packed and specimens can be kept small enough to remain in the windowbox permanently. Another plant that produces a symmetrical outline and that also does well in containers is the cabbage palm, *Cordyline australis*. Unlike box, this produces an airy fountain-shaped spray of foliage.

3 Cover the gravel with potting mix and then try the largest plant in the trough for size. Adjust the level accordingly. Leave a gap between the soil surface and rim of the liner so that water has a chance to soak in.

4 With the clipped box sphere in position in the center of the box, arrange the marguerites evenly so that they fill the two empty halves.

5 Use small pots of the silver-gray-leaved trailer Plecostachys serpyllifolia *(commonly sold in garden centers as Helichrysum microphyllum)* to soften the edge of the box.

6 Plant a couple of pots of white-variegated ivy at either end of the windowbox. Choose a variety with finely cut foliage to match the delicacy of the marguerites and decorative molding.

Plecostachys serpyllifolia

Buxus sempervirens 'Suffruticosa' *(dwarf box). If you trimmed it before planting in spring, you need not do so again until late summer. Use secateurs or sheep shears.*

Argyranthemum frutescens *(marguerite)*

Hedera helix *cultivar (variegated ivy)*

7 Deadhead and trim back the marguerites and do not allow them to swamp the dwarf box sphere. Plecostachys will also need cutting back occasionally.

Index to Plants

Page numbers in **bold** indicate major text references. Page numbers in *italics* indicate captions and annotations to photographs. Other text entries are shown in normal type.

Credits

The majority of the photographs featured in this book have been taken by Neil Sutherland and are ©
Colour Library Books. The publishers wish to thank the following photographers for providing
additional photographs, credited here by page number and position on the page, i.e. (B)Bottom, (T)Top,
(C)Center, (BL)Bottom left, etc.

Pat Brindley: 50(TR)
Eric Crichton: Half-title page, 63(TC)
John Glover: 14, 35(TR), 49(BR), 88, 90(L, BR), 91(TL, BL)
S & O Mathews: 35(BR)
Clive Nichols: 37(TR), 49(CB), 51(TL, TR), 74(T, National Asthma Campaign Garden. Chelsea
1993, Designer Lucy Harrington), 75(TL), 81(CR Designer, Anthony Noel)
Photos Horticultural: 70(TL)
Harry Smith Horticultural Photographic Collection: 51(BR)

Acknowledgments

The publishers would like to thank the following people and organizations for their help:
Neil Allen; Clive Bowes; Bressingham Plant Center, Diss, Norfolk; Bridgemere Garden World,
Nantwich, Cheshire; Shelley and Jonathan Choat; Country Gardens at Chichester, West Sussex; Court
Lane Nursery, Hadlow College, Kent; Grosvenor Garden Center, Belgrave, Chester; Hillier Nurseries
(Winchester) Ltd., Romsey, Hampshire; Iden Croft Herbs, Staplehurst, Kent; Little Brook Fuchsias,
Hampshire; Murrells Nursery, Pulborough, West Sussex; T. H. Waters; Treasures of Tenbury Ltd.